Will It Waffle?

Will It Waffle?

53 Unexpected and Irresistible Recipes to Make in a Waffle Iron

DANIEL SHUMSKI
creator of waffleizer.com

WORKMAN PUBLISHING • NEW YORK

Library of Congress Cataloging-in-Publication Data is available.

ISBN 978-0-7611-7646-6

Design by Jean-Marc Troadec
Cover and interior photography by Maes Studio, Inc.
Food stylist: Cindy Melin
Prop stylist: Lorrie Jamiolkowski

Additional photography on pages 100, 176, and 180 by Lucy Schaeffer
Food stylist: Chris Lanier
Prop stylist: Sara Abalan

Images on pages xi, xii, 4, and 5 by CSA Images/B&W Engrave Ink Collection/Getty Images

Special thanks to Chef's Choice for providing the waffle makers that appear in the photographs in this book.

Workman books are available at special discounts when purchased in bulk for premiums and sales promotions as well as for fund-raising or educational use. Special editions or book excerpts can also be created to specification. For details, contact the Special Sales Director at the address below, or send an email to specialmarkets@workman.com.

Workman Publishing Co., Inc.
225 Varick Street
New York, NY 10014-4381
workman.com

WORKMAN is a registered trademark of Workman Publishing Co., Inc.

Printed in the United States of America
First printing September 2014

10 9 8 7 6 5 4 3 2 1

To my mom, to whom I owe
my first waffle iron and everything else

Acknowledgments

Part of writing this book was just me in the kitchen with a waffle iron or three. But if that's all there was to it, I might have gone nuts. So I'm grateful there were other people involved. I owe a debt of gratitude to the chefs named in this book for opening their kitchens to me, going along with my crazy schemes, and even contributing some of their own. My thanks also to readers of *Waffleizer* and my past blogs who helped this little project gain steam before it jumped from the Internet to the printed page, in particular to those who provided kind words and recipe feedback. (Sometimes those two things even overlapped!) Thanks to my editor, Megan Nicolay; to Liz Davis and the rest of the team at Workman; to Michael Maes and his photography studio; and to my agent, Stacey Glick. Thank you to my mom for her voluminous and valuable feedback; to Bryan Kelly for his endless patience and near-endless willingness to try waffled foodstuffs; to Kathy Skutecki for brainstorming and testing; to Melanie Rheinecker for her keen eye and wise counsel; and to Nicholas Day and Peter Klein for their support and encouragement. I can't imagine having done this without any of these people. I'm lucky I didn't have to.

Contents

Introduction

Y ou know how sometimes you go to bed with something on your mind and you think maybe a good night's sleep will clear your head?

For me, that something was waffles.

Well, really it was anything *but* waffles. I already knew waffle batter would work in the waffle iron, but I caught little glimpses of other things: a French toast recipe for the waffle iron . . . cookies with a waffle pattern on them . . . waffled bacon. It wasn't much to go on, but it was enough. I was obsessed. What else would work in the waffle iron?

The idea wouldn't quit me on its own, so I decided to do something about it. In the proud tradition—well, the tradition— of people with too much time on their hands, I took my obsession to the Internet and created the blog *Waffleizer*. Once the "Will It Waffle?" question was out there, people were hungry for answers. Suddenly, the humble waffle iron was capable of more than most people had imagined. Once, it was for making waffles. Now it was for making breakfast, lunch, dinner, and everything in between.

Forgotten waffle irons emerged from dusty cabinets. Neglected waffle makers earned permanent space on the counter. A breakfast specialist turned into an all-day multi-tasker. And I heard about it all. People wrote to tell me that I had made them fall in love with their waffle irons all over again. (What had caused the falling out in the first place?) They wrote to tell me they were seriously thinking about getting a waffle iron. (Really? Just seriously *thinking* about it? How about seriously doing it?) They wrote to suggest recipes.

There's something about waffle geometry and the transformative power of the waffle iron that turns a recipe into an adventure, and if there's one thing that's become clear to me, it's that I'm not the only one who finds the adventure irresistible.

Waffling is growing. For a long while, after I stopped blogging and while I was working on this book, I wasn't sure what to expect. Would waffling wane? I needn't have worried. Waffling did not stop. In fact, it spread.

And yet, there's still more work to be done. Long maligned as single-purpose appliances, waffle irons have a reputation to overcome and baggage to shed.

Counter space is tight, you say? I hear you. But that is most typically a thing said by people who don't use their waffle irons because, yes, counter space is too tight for things you don't use.

Can't afford to buy a waffle iron, you say? Fair enough. Here's a thought: You may well know people who have one but do not use it. Quick! Convince them to give it to you before they find this book. (If that doesn't work, check yard sales, online auctions, for-sale listings, and thrift stores. Or hint a lot around the holidays or your birthday.)

We have a lot of waffling to do. I'm almost done here. Let me leave you with this:

These pages are my answers to the question, "Will it waffle?" But my answers are just the beginning. By the end of this book, you will have the tools you need to continue to experiment and build your own recipes.

Muster your sense of culinary daring. We're going to see what the waffle iron can do.

Will It Waffle?

Chapter I

Tools, Techniques, and Recipe Notes

As with any new endeavor, there can be a bit of a learning curve with waffling. The good news is I've made many of the waffle messes already so you don't have to. Plus, there are some tricks of the trade, tools, and techniques that will set you on the fast track to success. Before you jump in, take a few minutes to read about what I've learned, consider the merits of various waffle irons, and discover a few pieces of equipment that will help you along.

Waffle Irons

Clearly, the most important (and, quite frankly, mandatory) piece of machinery to have on hand for any of the recipes in this book is a waffle iron.

Let's get one thing out of the way: When it comes to waffle *iron* vs. waffle *maker*, it's mostly a question of word choice. The exception belongs to old-time contraptions made of cast iron and used to make waffles over open flames and in wood-burning stoves. Those are true waffle irons. The rest could probably go either way. When it comes to terminology, I tend toward "waffle iron" for a simple reason: I am the waffle maker; the machine is the waffle iron.

The two basic categories of waffle iron are the Belgian and the standard. I own six waffle irons. This is something I am not always quick to admit to strangers, but you're holding this book so I feel like I can tell you. You need only one.

BELGIAN WAFFLE IRON: Belgian waffle irons have deeper and generally fewer divots than the standard kind. While this may mean that your food will come out bearing fewer of the distinctive waffle marks, it also means that the marks that are present will be more pronounced.

STANDARD WAFFLE IRON: The standard waffle iron produces the most divots, but they are shallower than those of Belgian models.

NOVELTY WAFFLE IRON: This category encompasses a wide range of waffle irons, everything from models that produce zoo-animal shapes, to waffle "sticks" with a single row of divots, to a particularly famous cartoon mouse, to the logo of your favorite sports team. The good news is that most of these will probably work with the recipes in this book, though in some cases it may involve some creative shaping to fit the food in the waffle iron.

Whether you use a Belgian or a standard is up to you. Some recipes in this book work slightly differently in each, but all have been tested with both. A few recipes come with notes on preparing them in one kind versus another. Whether Belgian or standard, waffle irons typically come in either round or rectangular shapes. In general, either one will work for the recipes in this book, though the results may of course look different from the photos.

Some waffle irons have temperature controls and some do not. The recipes in this book include recommended temperatures for waffle irons with temperature controls, but you should be able to make the recipes work even without temperature controls—though it may take some experimentation.

Useful Tools

Most waffling doesn't require any special equipment beyond a waffle iron. There are a few tools that will come in handy, though.

SILICONE SPATULA(S): Silicone withstands the high heat of your waffle iron and avoids the danger of scraping with metal utensils, which can scratch nonstick coatings. Use a spatula to flip and turn hot food.

Having two means you can use them as tongs to lift out food from the waffle iron (or, invest in silicone-tipped tongs to pair with your spatula).

SILICONE PASTRY BRUSH(ES): Unlike a traditional brush, which can leave behind boar- or horse-hair bristles in your food, silicone bristles are firmly attached to the brush head. Use a brush to coat food or the waffle iron with butter or oil.

COOLING RACK: Piping-hot food needs air circulating around it so that it can cool quickly and evenly.

SPONGE CLOTH(S): Burnt bits in the crevices of your waffle iron are inevitable. Flexible, thick, reusable sponge cloths let you clean in the corners.

INSTANT-READ DIGITAL THERMOMETER: This comes in handy not just for waffling, but for cooking all kinds of meat, as well as for making jam, candy, and countless other things. If you don't have one of these, there might be a little guesswork and slicing involved to see whether your food is done.

GREAT MOMENTS IN WAFFLING

ANCIENT GREECE	MEDIEVAL EUROPE	16TH-CENTURY FRANCE
### THE MOTHER OF ALL WAFFLES	### I SAW JESUS IN MY WAFFLE!	### THE AWFUL WAFFLE KERFUFFLE
In Ancient Greece, bakers cooked savory flat cakes called *obelios* between two hot plates. It's the oldest known ancestor of the modern waffle.	Medieval waffle irons were engraved with religious iconography and used for communion. Until merchants started selling waffles, they intentionally tasted plain.	Legend has it that in 16th-century France, waffle vendors had grown so numerous and boisterous at religious holidays that King Charles IX had to create a law keeping waffle stands a certain distance from each other.

The Care and Handling of Your Waffle Iron

Waffle irons are fairly foolproof when it comes to making standard breakfast waffles, but when you dabble beyond that, there are special considerations. Before you start, here are a (very) few things to keep in mind.

HOW TO KEEP YOUR WAFFLE IRON CLEAN

There's no doubt, waffling can get messy—as all great experiments/ art can. The key is being prepared and taking a few steps beforehand that can make cleanup easier. If you end up with a mess on your hands despite your best efforts, don't worry. There are some easy ways to clean up your waffle iron and get back in business. Before you waffle, keep the following in mind:

1. Use the nonstick spray or oil recommended in the recipe to ensure the food lifts cleanly from the waffle iron.

2. Lay down newspaper under the waffle iron. If anything spills or overflows, you can clean up by disposing of the newspaper.

1620	1789	1820s
TURKEY, GRAVY, PUMPKIN PIE, WAFFLES	*CAVORTING WITH WAFFLES*	*THE CLOSEST WE'LL GET TO WAFFLING ICE CREAM*
After a pit stop in the Netherlands, pilgrims brought the first waffles to the New World in 1620.	In 1789, Thomas Jefferson returned from France bearing, among other treasures, a waffle iron. This is said to have briefly revived a pre-colonial tradition of Dutch settlers: social gatherings based on waffles called "waffle frolics."	While the concept of edible, waffle-like treat holders is recorded as far back as the 1820s, Italo Marconi received the first patent for the ice cream cone in 1903.

A lucky few of you may have waffle irons with removable grids, which make cleanup easier. If not, one of the best methods for cleaning your waffle iron is also the most delicious: Make standard waffles. The first waffle may be a bit of a sacrifice, as leftover food from the last waffling project gets absorbed into the batter. But when you lift out that first waffle, you'll lift out with it any lingering burnt bits from previous projects. Problem solved. (And if the lingering bits are, say, bacon or sausage, it may be your duty to eat said waffle.)

If making waffles isn't an option, two methods produce similar results:

1. Make a simple batter from equal parts flour and water and cook it in the waffle iron for 4 to 6 minutes, or until it holds together well enough to be lifted out. Again, any lingering bits get cooked into the batter and are lifted out when it is removed.

2. If you have leftover grease in the waffle iron, you can sacrifice some inexpensive sandwich bread to clean it. Place a few slices in the waffle iron and close the lid. The bread will absorb most of the grease. Then wipe down the grid with a paper towel dampened in a weak vinegar solution (1 cup water mixed with 1 tablespoon white vinegar).

1869   **1938**

WAFFLES MADE EASY!

The stovetop waffle iron was patented by Dutch American inventor Cornelius Swarthout on August 24, 1869; the anniversary is still celebrated as National Waffle Day.

HOLIDAYS ARE NICE, BUT PUN-BASED HOLIDAYS ARE BATTER

International Waffle Day, on the other hand, is March 25, grown from a Swedish pun. There's a religious holiday on March 25 called Vårfrudagen, which means "Our Lady's Day" but sounds remarkably similar to Våffeldagen, which means "Waffle Day."

BREAKFAST AND DINNER IN ONE MEAL!

The combination of chicken and waffles is recorded as far back as the 17th century and was popularized in 1938 by Harlem's Wells Supper Club, patronized by the likes of Nat King Cole and Sammy Davis Jr.

If there are some dry bits of food remaining in the waffle iron, try the following, continuing through the steps until the waffle iron is clean:

1. With the waffle iron off and cooled, stand the machine sideways on newspaper and brush off the crumbs.

2. For getting in the nooks and crannies without scratching a nonstick surface, try poking around with some wooden chopsticks from your last order of takeout.

3. With the waffle iron off, use a soft toothbrush to scrape up any burnt bits. (Obviously, you're using either a toothbrush dedicated to this or one belonging to someone you don't like.) For an extra boost, make a paste of 4 parts baking soda to 1 part water and use the toothbrush to apply.

4. With the waffle iron on low, place a clean, wet dishtowel in the waffle iron for a minute. The steam will help loosen any stuck-on bits.

5. With the waffle iron off, pour a bit of seltzer water on the grid and use paper towels or a dishtowel to wipe clean.

1953	1955	1964
GET OFF(LE) MY FROFFLE!	**YOUR MIDNIGHT WAFFLE FIX**	**THEY SURE BEAT BRUSSELS SPROUTS**
In 1953, the world was introduced to Froffles, short for frozen waffles. After customers noted their eggy taste, creators Frank, Sam, and Tony Dorsa changed their brand's name to Eggo.	Waffle House opened its doors outside Atlanta on September 5, 1955, and has yet to close them: The diner chain is open 24 hours a day, every day of the year.	The Belgian waffle was brought to the United States at the New York World's Fair in 1964 by Brussels restaurateur Maurice Vermersch, based on a recipe that his wife concocted during World War II.

WAFFLE IRON SAFETY AND STORAGE

See your waffle iron's manual for details on safety considerations for your model, but in general remember that the metal surfaces of your waffle iron will get quite hot. Always approach and handle the waffle iron as though it might be hot. Do not store the waffle iron until it has fully cooled.

Recipe Notes

Most of these recipes will work in just about any kind of electric waffle maker, whether Belgian-style or standard, square, round, or heart-shaped. That said, each recipe notes any special considerations for one style of machine or another.

One important note: As mentioned in the Waffle Irons section, not all waffle makers have temperature controls. The recipes include a recommended temperature, but even among waffle makers with temperature controls, the temperatures may vary. If yours doesn't have temperature settings, don't worry. The recipes will still work. You may need to keep a close eye on things until you understand how your waffle iron behaves.

1960s	1972	1979
POLITICAL WAFFLING	**WILL IT WAFFLE?: INEDIBLE EDITION**	**A WAFFLE IMPOSTOR**
In the 1960s, a Canadian socialist group called "The Waffle Movement" was formed. (Alas, it was named for the verb, not the food.)	In 1972, Blue Ribbon Sports began selling Moon Shoes, featuring unique tread soles created by inventor Bill Bowerman pouring liquid rubber in his wife's waffle iron. Blue Ribbon would later change its name to Nike.	In October 1979, Edgar Matsler patented a potato slicer that brought us waffle fries. Tragically, their similarity to waffles is limited to appearance.

With or without temperature controls, there's one key question to sort out before you begin: How do you know when your waffle iron is preheated and ready to waffle? I've seen some waffle irons where a light goes *on* when they finish preheating, and waffle irons where a light goes *off* when they finish preheating. Some beep loudly when they come to temperature. Some are silent. The best thing to do is to consult the manual that came with your waffle iron. If that is long gone or so stained in maple syrup as to be illegible, then allow 10 minutes for your waffle iron to preheat.

Needless to say, your waffle iron's temperature will affect how long it takes for something to cook. So pay attention to the cooking times given in the recipes, but don't abide by them absolutely. They're based on tests using various waffle irons but not *your* waffle iron. More than the estimated time, pay attention to the expected result (and temperature in some cases). If the recipe says the dish is ready when it is golden brown and the cheese is melted, that's what you're looking for—regardless of what the timer says.

Lastly, remember that you can't uncook food. Once it's burned, it's burned. Err on the side of caution and check on the early side of the recommended times at first. The more you work with your waffle iron, the more you'll understand its quirks and tendencies. You might make mistakes along the way, but most of your mistakes will be the best kind of mistakes: edible ones.

2010	2012	2013
UNLAWFUL WAFFLE USAGE	**A SHOT OF BREAKFAST**	**WILL IT WAFFLE?: SOLVING WORLD HUNGER EDITION**
In 2010, fans of the Toronto Maple Leafs vented their disappointment with the team's poor performance by hurling waffles at the players.	On August 24, 2012—the 143rd anniversary of Cornelius Swarthout's stovetop waffle iron—New York City–based alcohol producer Georgi introduced the world to waffle-flavored vodka. No word on how well it goes with syrup.	On June 29, 2013, Netherlands native Stichting Gouda Oogst baked the first waffle to top 50 kilograms (roughly 110 pounds). With a diameter spanning more than eight feet, it earned the Guinness World Record for the world's largest waffle.

Chapter 2
Breakfast and Brunch

Crispy Waffled Bacon and Eggs

IRON: Belgian or standard | **TIME:** 10 minutes | **YIELD:** Serves 2

Cooking the eggs in the bacon drippings is just one bonus to this method.

INGREDIENTS

4 strips bacon

2 large eggs

Salt and freshly ground black pepper, to taste

Bacon cooked in a frying pan is quick. The downside? It sizzles and can send grease flying in all directions—especially in whichever direction your hand happens to be. Bacon cooked in the oven saves you from flying bits of grease but takes longer.

There is another consideration when seeking bacon perfection: For me, the ideal cooking method makes the bacon crispy.

So what we're after is some way to combine the speed of the frying pan with the relative neatness of the oven.

What we're after is the waffle iron.

1 Preheat the waffle iron on medium. Preheat the oven on its lowest setting. Line a plate with paper towels.

2 Place the bacon strips in the waffle iron and close the lid. Make sure the bacon is not hanging out of the sides of the waffle iron.

3 Check after 4 minutes. Thin-cut bacon could be ready, though thicker cuts may need another 1 to 2 minutes. Bacon is ready when it is crispy without being blackened.

4 Remove the bacon and drain it on the paper towel–lined plate to absorb some of the grease.

(While you cook the eggs, the waffled bacon can be kept warm on a baking sheet in the oven.)

5 Crack the eggs into a small bowl. This will give you control over how the eggs land on the waffle iron. The waffle iron should be well greased from cooking the bacon, but if necessary, use a silicone pastry brush to distribute the bacon fat evenly across the portion of the waffle iron where the eggs will cook.

6 Pour the eggs onto the greased part of the waffle iron.

Cook, without closing the lid, until the egg white has set, about a minute, and continue cooking until the yolk has set a bit, 1 or 2 minutes more.

7 To remove the eggs intact, use an offset spatula or a pair of heat-resistant silicone spatulas to coax them from the grid of the waffle iron. Loosen the edges first and then lift out the egg while supporting it from below as much as possible.

8 Season with salt and pepper and serve with the waffled bacon.

Sweet and Savory Waffled Sausage Patties

IRON: Belgian or standard | **TIME:** 15 minutes | **YIELD:** Serves 6

In which maple syrup and sage pork sausage make the perfect marriage.

The first time I traveled to Canada, I saw maple everywhere. There's the leaf on the flag, of course—but also the cans of syrup stacked up in grocery stores, the candies in the convenience stores, the pastries in the bakery windows, and the cookbooks in the gift shops.

Some time later, I ended up moving there and found myself, as one does, wanting to make a sausage homage to my new home. So I incorporated a little maple syrup into my favorite sausage recipe and crossed my fingers that it would work in the waffle iron. I needn't have worried. It worked beautifully.

Make these for breakfast and follow them up with a round of Buttermilk Cornmeal Waffles (page 187). The waffles will pick up some of the drippings from the sausage.

INGREDIENTS

2 tablespoons maple syrup

1 teaspoon dried sage

1 teaspoon salt

½ teaspoon freshly ground black pepper

¼ teaspoon dried marjoram

⅛ teaspoon cayenne pepper

1 pound ground pork

Nonstick cooking spray

NOTE: Grade A is for syrup with lighter color and more straightforward sweetness, while Grade B syrup is darker and has a more pronounced maple flavor (my personal preference).

1 Preheat the waffle iron on medium. Preheat the oven on its lowest setting.

2 In a medium-size bowl, combine the maple syrup, sage, salt, black pepper, marjoram, and cayenne pepper and mix well to combine.

3 Add the pork to the spice mixture, and mix well with your hands. Form patties that will fit on one section of your waffle iron.

4 Coat both sides of the waffle iron grid with nonstick spray. Place a patty on each section of the waffle iron and close the lid. With thin patties in a conventional-style waffle iron, the meat may be done in as little as 2 minutes. Belgian-style machines or thicker patties may require more time. The pork should reach an internal temperature of 160°F on an instant-read thermometer.

5 Remove the patties from the waffle iron and serve. Place the finished sausage patties in the oven to keep them warm while the others cook in the waffle iron.

VARIATION

Substitute an equal amount of reduced apple cider for the maple syrup. To make reduced apple cider: In a saucepan, simmer a quart of apple cider over low heat, stirring occasionally, until it thickens and becomes syrupy. The cider may take about an hour to reduce, but pay more attention to its texture than the clock. Store the reduced cider in a glass container in the refrigerator for up to a month and use it on pancakes, waffles, and ice cream.

Waffled Chocolate-Stuffed French Toast
with Whipped Butter

IRON: Belgian or standard │ **TIME:** 20 minutes │ **YIELD:** Serves 2

An embedded layer of chocolate and whipped butter topping elevate the French toast experience.

Waffled French toast was a big hit when I first made it. At its simplest, the same ingredients you'd use to prepare normal French toast are prepared in the waffle iron. And that's great.

But as an inveterate tinkerer, I had to ask myself: How could it be even better? Adding chocolate is a good bet, but adding the chocolate on the outside would risk burning it. Building the chocolate component *between* the two slices, however, means the bread insulates the chocolate from the direct heat of the waffle iron, thus melting it without scorching it.

Oh, but there's another potential snag: Waffling can be a squishy business. You pile the ingredients into the waffle iron, close the lid, and watch as the lid presses down, down, down. As the food cooks, the lid sinks. Your creation comes out waffled, yes—but the chocolate layer also comes out thin. The solution (as with so many things):

INGREDIENTS

2 large eggs

½ cup milk

¼ teaspoon pure
vanilla extract

Pinch of salt

4 slices bread, such as
challah or brioche,
cut thick

Nonstick cooking spray

½ cup chocolate chips
(semisweet, bittersweet,
or milk chocolate)

1 tablespoon Whipped
Butter (recipe follows)

Powdered sugar, to taste

Add more chocolate. A few chocolate chips stuffed into the pocket of the finished product melt in no time from the residual heat.

The French toast comes out gorgeously gooey, rich, and delicious.

I Preheat the waffle iron on high. Preheat the oven on its lowest setting.

2 In a pie pan or deep dish, whisk together the eggs, milk, vanilla, and salt.

3 Place 2 slices of bread in the egg mixture and soak them until they've absorbed some of the liquid, 30 seconds. Flip the slices and soak them for another 30 seconds.

4 Coat both sides of the waffle iron grid with nonstick spray. Place a slice of soaked bread on the waffle iron and pile a little less than half of the chocolate chips on the slice. Top with the second slice of soaked bread, close the waffle iron, and cook until the bread is golden brown and the chocolate is melted, 3 to 4 minutes. There should be no trace of uncooked egg mixture.

5 Remove the French toast from the waffle iron and repeat Steps 3 and 4 to make the second batch. Place the finished French toast in the oven to keep it warm.

6 Slice the French toast into quarters. Pop open the "pocket" in each quarter and stuff the remaining chocolate chips into the opening. The residual heat will melt the chocolate.

7 Top each portion with the Whipped Butter and dust with the powdered sugar before serving.

VARIATIONS

Replace half of the chocolate chips in Step 4 with ¼ cup of any of these ingredients:

- Mascarpone cheese
- Peach, apricot, or cherry jam
- Orange or lemon marmalade
- Dulce de leche
- Peanut butter
- Fresh raspberries
- Slices of banana

Whipped Butter

Whipped butter adds a restaurant-quality touch to the dish. It's best to use salted butter. To make whipped butter, set out the butter at room temperature for 1 hour to allow it to soften. Once it has softened, put it in a mixing bowl and beat with an electric mixer on medium speed until the butter is fluffy and slightly lighter in color, 1 minute.

INGREDIENTS

8 tablespoons (1 stick) salted butter

NOTE: To make citrus-flavored whipped butter, add 1 teaspoon orange or lemon zest per ½ cup butter.

Blueberry Cinnamon Muffles (Waffled Muffins)

IRON: Belgian or standard (Belgian allows for fluffier muffles) | **TIME:** 20 minutes | **YIELD:** About 16 muffles

Half waffle and half muffin, these taste even better than the sum of their parts.

These may earn a permanent spot in your breakfast repertoire. They have in mine. Wild blueberries work best not just because they tend to be more intensely flavored, but also because they tend to be smaller. If a blueberry comes into contact with the direct heat of the waffle iron, the sugars may burn and leave you with a dark splotch in your waffled blueberry muffin. The larger the blueberry, the larger the splotch.

The recipe will work with fresh blueberries, but, most of the year, frozen blueberries are a better bet for both price and flavor.

1 Preheat the waffle iron on medium.

2 In a medium-size bowl, combine the flour, sugar, cinnamon, salt, and baking powder.

3 In a large bowl, combine the milk, butter, and eggs and whisk until thoroughly combined.

4 Add the dry ingredients to the milk mixture and whisk until just combined.

5 Fold in the blueberries and stir gently to distribute them evenly.

6 Coat both sides of the waffle iron grid with nonstick spray and pour about ¼ cup of the mixture into each section of the waffle iron. Close the lid and cook for 4 minutes, or until just golden brown.

7 Remove the muffles from the waffle iron, and let them cool slightly on a wire rack. Repeat Step 6 with the remaining batter.

8 Serve warm.

INGREDIENTS

2 cups all-purpose flour

¼ cup granulated sugar

1 teaspoon ground cinnamon

½ teaspoon salt

2 teaspoons baking powder

2 cups milk, at room temperature

8 tablespoons (1 stick) unsalted butter, melted

2 large eggs

1 cup frozen wild blueberries

Nonstick cooking spray

NOTE: Using milk at room temperature means the melted butter won't clump up when it is mixed with the milk.

TIPS

• Any remaining batter can be refrigerated and cooked the next day according to the instructions above. Allow a minute more in the waffle iron to account for the cold batter.

• Cooked muffles can be stored in a zip-top bag in the freezer and reheated in the waffle iron on medium heat for 2 minutes.

Waffled Ham and Cheese Melt with Maple Butter

IRON: Belgian or standard | **TIME:** 10 minutes | **YIELD:** Serves 1

Use real maple syrup here, and don't be shy about serving a little on the side for dipping.

INGREDIENTS

1 tablespoon unsalted butter, at room temperature

2 slices sandwich bread

2 ounces Gruyère cheese, sliced

3 ounces Black Forest ham, sliced

1 tablespoon Maple Butter (recipe follows)

When I first dreamed up this sandwich, I wanted the maple butter to go on the bread *before* it went into the waffle iron, but that turned out to be a recipe for disaster: The sugars in the maple syrup burned quickly, much more quickly than the cheese melted. There would have to be another way. And there is! After a few modifications, I hit on the right balance of pre- and post-buttering.

There's still room for pre-buttering, just hold the maple syrup on that step. Buttering the bread before you waffle it ensures a crispy, golden brown exterior. Adding the maple butter right as the sandwich comes out of the waffle iron means the sweet, rich mixture soaks into the still-warm bread.

1 Preheat the waffle iron on low.

2 Spread a thin, even layer of butter on one side of each piece of bread.

3 Pile the cheese and ham on the unbuttered side of one slice of bread, and put the open-face sandwich in the waffle iron as far away from the hinge as

possible. (This allows the lid to press down on the sandwich more evenly.) Place the second slice of bread on top, with the buttered side up, and close the waffle iron.

4 Check the sandwich after 3 minutes. About halfway through, you may need to rotate the sandwich 180 degrees to ensure even pressure and cooking. If you'd like, you can press down on the lid of the waffle iron a bit to compact the sandwich, but do so carefully— the lid could be very hot. Remove the sandwich from the waffle iron when the bread is golden brown and the cheese is melted.

5 Spread the Maple Butter on the outside of the sandwich. Slice in half diagonally and serve.

INGREDIENTS

8 tablespoons (1 stick) salted butter, at room temperature

1 tablespoon maple syrup

NOTE: You'll have leftover maple butter, which can be stored in a covered container in the refrigerator, where it will keep at least a month. Here's what to do with the extra maple butter: Allow it to come to room temperature before serving it on sweet potatoes, French toast, pancakes, or . . . waffles.

Maple Butter

Combine the ingredients in a medium-size bowl and whip with an electric mixer or a whisk until well blended.

Waffled Hash Browns
with Rosemary

IRON: Belgian or standard | **TIME:** 20 minutes | **YIELD:** Serves 2

If I ever open a diner, these are going on the menu. Nothing else. Just these.

You know how when you cook potatoes on the stove top or in the oven you have to stir them to make sure they brown on all sides? Cooking potatoes in the waffle iron ensures that the potato is crisp on both sides without any need for flipping.

Here's what I learned: Don't slice the potatoes, shred them. I tried slicing. Putting sliced potatoes in the waffle iron gives you limp potatoes that don't come together, and they emerge with few signs of being waffled. This was true whether I used raw potatoes or parboiled potatoes. Shredding the potatoes results in a fantastic amount of crunch on the outside and tiny pockets of silky smooth potato inside.

And once you're in on that secret, it couldn't be easier.

1 Preheat the waffle iron on medium.

2 Squeeze the shredded potato with a towel until it's as dry as you can manage. (Excess liquid is the enemy of crispiness; your potatoes will steam if they aren't dried well.)

3 In a mixing bowl, combine the shredded potato, rosemary, salt, and pepper.

4 With a silicone brush, spread the butter on both sides of the waffle iron.

5 Pile the shredded potatoes into the waffle iron—overstuff the waffle iron a bit—and close

INGREDIENTS

1 russet (baking) potato, about 10 ounces, peeled and shredded

$\frac{1}{2}$ teaspoon finely chopped fresh rosemary or 1 teaspoon dried rosemary

$\frac{1}{4}$ teaspoon salt

$\frac{1}{2}$ teaspoon freshly ground black pepper

1 teaspoon unsalted butter, melted

Grated cheese, sour cream, or ketchup, for serving

the lid. (The pressure of the lid will compress the potatoes and help them emerge as a cohesive, waffled unit.)

6 After 2 minutes, press down a bit on the lid to further compress the potatoes. (Careful: The lid may be hot.) Check the potatoes after 10 minutes. They should be just starting to turn golden brown in places.

7 When the potatoes are golden brown throughout, 1 to 2 minutes more, carefully remove them from the waffle iron.

8 Serve with grated cheese, sour cream, or ketchup.

Truffled Eggs,
Scrambled and Waffled

IRON: Belgian or standard | **TIME:** 5 minutes | **YIELD:** Serves 1

In a few minutes, you can have beautifully scrambled eggs—pillowy, rich, and perfect for the weekend.

These are not everyday scrambled eggs. They're decadent. This recipe calls for butter, not nonstick spray. It calls for cream, not milk. Most important, it calls for truffle oil. Truffle oil is usually in the neighborhood of 99 percent olive oil infused with a bit of truffle flavor. Even a little bit of it will impart the earthy, incomparable flavor of truffles. After you've used a teaspoon in this recipe, try it in mashed potatoes, on pasta, or even over popcorn. It's expensive, yes, but it's cheaper than buying raw truffles or renting a pig and searching for your own.

INGREDIENTS

2 large eggs

1 tablespoon heavy (whipping) cream

1 teaspoon black truffle–infused oil

Pinch of salt

Pinch of freshly ground black pepper

1 tablespoon melted butter, for brushing waffle iron

When you pour the eggs onto the waffle iron, you may think they're going to stick. After a few minutes, you may still worry they're going to stick. Just follow the instructions and keep stirring. As long as you've generously buttered the waffle iron, the eggs should pull away from the waffle iron grid as they cook.

1 Preheat the waffle iron on medium.

2 In a medium-size bowl, whisk the eggs with the cream until just combined.

3 Add the truffle oil, salt, and pepper, and whisk again to combine.

4 Use a silicone brush to generously coat the bottom grid of the waffle iron with butter.

5 Pour the eggs onto the waffle iron and leave the lid open.

6 Using a silicone spatula, stir the eggs frequently while they cook. The trick here is to move the eggs out of the crevices so that the uncooked egg can come into contact with the waffle iron and cook thoroughly.

7 Keep a close eye on the eggs. They may be done in as little as 2 minutes, though they may take up to 3 minutes. No runny parts should remain.

8 Remove the eggs from the waffle iron with an offset spatula or a pair of heat-resistant silicone spatulas. Loosen the edges first and then lift out the eggs while supporting them from below as much as possible. Serve hot.

VARIATIONS

Instead of truffle oil, add:

- A handful of chopped fresh herbs, such as dill, chives, or parsley

- 1 ounce finely chopped smoked salmon

Chapter 3
Main
Courses

Gridded Grilled Cheese

IRON: Belgian or standard | **TIME:** 5 minutes | **YIELD:** Serves 1

You probably already have the ingredients to make this, so what are you waiting for?

Grilled cheese and waffles, separately, are two childhood favorites. Now that you're an adult, you can play with your food and make them one. Adding the waffle iron to the mix gives grilled cheese a little twist without changing either of the fundamentals that make it a classic—the melty, gooey cheese and the buttery, toasted bread. If you're adventurous, you can jazz up the sandwich. And you should, right after you make your first plain old waffled grilled cheese.

1 Preheat the waffle iron on low.

2 Butter one side of each slice of bread.

3 Place a slice of bread, buttered side down, on the waffle iron, as far away from the hinge as possible. (This will allow the lid to press down on the sandwich more evenly.) Distribute the cheese evenly on the bread. Top with the second slice of bread, buttered side up.

4 Close the lid of the waffle iron and cook until the cheese is melted and the bread is golden brown, 3 minutes. About halfway through, you may need to rotate the sandwich 180 degrees to ensure even pressure and cooking.

5 Remove the sandwich from the waffle iron. Slice into halves or quarters and serve.

INGREDIENTS

1 tablespoon unsalted butter, at room temperature

2 slices sturdy sandwich bread

3 ounces cheese, such as Cheddar or Taleggio, thinly sliced (see Tip, page 38)

NOTE: Flimsy sandwich bread may not stand up to the heat of the cheese and the waffle iron. Choose something with a little heft, maybe a nice solid rye bread, or a multigrain that's not too spongy. For a richer sandwich, use brioche or challah.

VARIATIONS

For a twist on the traditional grilled cheese, try adding one or two of the following:

• Tomatoes, thinly sliced • Apple or pear, thinly sliced • Jalapeño peppers, finely chopped • Bacon or bacon bits • Baby spinach • Jam • Onion • Dijon mustard

Green Chile Waffled Quesadillas

IRON: Belgian or standard | **TIME:** 10 minutes | **YIELD:** Makes 2 quesadillas

waffled quesadillas are versatile and unfussy— perfect for a weeknight dinner.

Quesadillas are practically made for the waffle iron. Or . . . are waffle irons practically made for quesadillas? Either way, the two-sided heat and the compression of the waffle iron make for a quick and impressive meal.

INGREDIENTS

Nonstick cooking spray

4 flour tortillas

1 cup shredded Mexican-style cheese, such as queso Chihuahua or Monterey Jack

¼ cup chopped canned green chiles

NOTE: Leftover green chiles can be placed in a zip-top bag and frozen. Stir into omelets or cornbread, or use them to top a cheeseburger.

Quesadillas make the perfect vessel for leftovers, too. They embrace customization and accommodate whatever you have in your fridge. Those bits of chicken or turkey? They'll fit right in. Some left-over roasted vegetables? They'll go nicely, too. It'll be almost like you planned it this way.

As the cheese melts, some will inevitably escape from the tortillas. Make the most of this. Use a heatproof spatula to scrape off the crispy cheese from the grid, chop it up, and sprinkle it atop the finished quesadillas as a garnish.

I Preheat the waffle iron on medium. Coat both sides of the waffle iron grid with nonstick spray.

2 Place a tortilla on the waffle iron and, taking care because the waffle iron is hot, spread half of the cheese and half of the green chiles evenly across the tortilla, leaving a margin of an inch or so around the edge of the tortilla. Top with another tortilla and close the waffle iron.

3 Check the quesadilla after 3 minutes. When the cheese is melted and the tortilla has golden brown waffle marks, it is ready. Remove the quesadilla from the waffle iron.

4 Repeat Steps 2 and 3 with the remaining ingredients, cut into wedges, and serve.

VARIATIONS

For a more substantial meal, add one of the following to the tortilla in Step 2:

- ½ cup shredded chicken or pork
- ½ cup sliced steak
- ½ cup refried beans

Garnish with one or more of the following:

- Chopped scallion
- Crumbled bacon
- Sour cream
- Salsa
- Guacamole

WBLT
(Waffled Bacon, Lettuce, and Tomato)

IRON: Belgian or standard | **TIME:** 10 minutes | **YIELD:** Serves 1

For a more colorful sandwich, try heirloom tomatoes such as Green Zebra, Tigerella, or Cherokee Purple.

This is perfect for the peak of summer, when tomatoes are at their best and turning on the oven is unthinkable.

Waffling the bacon first means that a little bacon grease gets into the bread when you assemble the sandwich and waffle it. Spreading the bread with softened butter helps it along, making sure the bread toasts evenly.

1 Preheat the waffle iron on medium.

2 Place the bacon strips in the waffle iron and close the lid. To ensure the bacon cooks thoroughly and evenly, make sure no part of the bacon is hanging out of the waffle iron.

3 After 4 minutes, check the bacon—thin-cut slices could be ready, though thicker cuts may need 1 or 2 minutes more. When the bacon is crispy without being blackened, remove it from the waffle iron and set aside. Turn the waffle iron down to low.

4 Spread a thin, even layer of butter on one side of each piece of bread. Spread the mayonnaise on the other side of one slice of bread and place it—mayo side up—on the waffle

INGREDIENTS

3 strips bacon

1 tablespoon unsalted butter, at room temperature

2 slices sturdy sandwich bread

2 teaspoons mayonnaise

1 small ripe tomato, cut into ½-inch-thick slices

2 leaves lettuce, washed and dried completely

iron, as far away from the hinge as possible. (This allows the lid to press down on the sandwich more evenly.) Distribute the bacon, tomato, and lettuce evenly across the sandwich. Top with the second slice of bread, butter side up.

5 Close the lid of the waffle iron and cook until the bread is golden brown, 2 minutes. About halfway through, you may need to rotate the sandwich 180 degrees to ensure even pressure and cooking.

6 Remove the sandwich, slice it in half diagonally, and serve.

VARIATIONS

- Add a slice of ripe avocado.
- Substitute arugula for the lettuce.
- Substitute smoked salmon for the cooked bacon.
- Add a sliced hard-boiled egg.
- Substitute roasted red pepper slices for the tomato.
- Substitute a thin layer of pesto for the mayonnaise.

Waffled Cuban Sandwich

| **IRON:** Belgian or standard | **TIME:** 10 minutes | **YIELD:** Serves 2 |

For a complete meal, serve this sandwich with waffled Tostones (page 148).

INGREDIENTS

1 crusty sandwich roll or individual ciabatta loaf

1 tablespoon yellow mustard

3 ounces cooked ham, thinly sliced

3 ounces cooked pork loin, thinly sliced

3 ounces Swiss cheese, thinly sliced

2 dill pickles, thinly sliced lengthwise

TIP

Before you waffle, size up your waffle iron and your bread. If the sandwich is going to be a tight squeeze, the solution is simple: Assemble it first, split it into two parts, and waffle one part at a time.

This sandwich is a pork-laden monstrosity that mixes things up with some cheese and pickle for good measure. It is traditionally served pressed, which makes it a perfect candidate for being waffled.

Testing proved that hollowing out the bread was the best way to make sure the sandwich compressed neatly. There's only so much room in the waffle iron and something had to give. Leaving the bread intact just didn't allow enough space for the ingredients.

1 Preheat the waffle iron on low.

2 Split the bread into top and bottom halves, hollow it out a bit to make room for the meat, and spread the mustard across both slices. Assemble the ham, pork loin, cheese, and pickles between the pieces of bread.

3 Press down on the sandwich to compact it a bit and place it in the waffle iron, as far away from the hinge as possible. (This allows the lid to press down on the sandwich more evenly.)

4 Close the lid of the waffle iron and cook for 5 minutes. About halfway through, you may need to rotate the sandwich 180 degrees to ensure even pressure and cooking. If you'd like, you can press down on the lid of the waffle iron a bit to compact the sandwich, but do so carefully—the lid could be very hot.

5 Remove the sandwich from the waffle iron when the cheese is thoroughly melted. Cut the sandwich in half, or diagonally, and serve.

Waffled Gyro
with Tzatziki Sauce

IRON: Belgian or standard | **TIME:** 45 minutes | **YIELD:** Serves 4

warm the pita bread in the waffle iron to waffle this gyro inside and out.

How do you translate something traditionally roasted on a spit to the waffle iron?

You start with lamb—not strips of meat, but ground meat. Then there are the spices—a blend that is complex but still a little forgiving. It's a long list of spices, but if you're missing one, don't run out to the store. It will taste a little different, sure, but there's a lot going on here, and it won't be missed too much. The meat mixture is spicy, but the yogurt sauce and cucumber have a cooling effect that brings everything into balance.

Prepare the tzatziki sauce first so the flavors have time to meld while you prepare the meat. The recipe calls for two cloves of garlic, but the best idea is to add only one at first and taste it before you add the second one. The first time I made this, the garlic cloves were enormous. It was too much. And once it's in there, it's in there. Better to add a bit at a time.

INGREDIENTS

Tzatziki sauce:

2 cloves garlic,
  finely minced

16 ounces plain Greek
  yogurt

1 medium-size cucumber,
  peeled, seeded, and
  finely chopped

1 tablespoon extra-virgin
  olive oil

2 teaspoons white vinegar

Pinch of kosher salt

Gyros:

1 tablespoon dried parsley

1 teaspoon chili powder

1 teaspoon ground coriander

1 teaspoon ground cumin

1 teaspoon dried oregano

1 teaspoon dried thyme

½ teaspoon paprika

½ teaspoon garlic powder

½ teaspoon ground
  cinnamon

½ teaspoon salt

1 pound lean ground lamb

Nonstick cooking spray

4 pita bread pockets

1 medium-size tomato,
  cut into cubes

1 medium-size onion,
  thinly sliced

1 Make the sauce: In a medium-size bowl, combine half of the garlic with the remaining ingredients and stir well. Taste and add more garlic, if desired. Refrigerate the sauce for at least 30 minutes while you prepare the gyros.

2 Preheat the waffle iron on medium.

3 Make the gyros: In a large bowl, combine the parsley, chili powder, coriander, cumin, oregano, thyme, paprika, garlic powder, cinnamon, and salt and then add the meat to the spice mixture. Mix well to distribute the spices evenly.

4 Form the spiced lamb into 4 patties. Coat both sides of the waffle iron grid with nonstick spray.

5 Place a patty on the waffle iron, close the lid, and cook until no traces of pink remain, 4 minutes. If you're using an instant-read thermometer, the internal temperature of the lamb should reach 160°F. Repeat for the remaining patties.

6 When all of the lamb patties have finished cooking, warm the pita bread for 15 seconds in the waffle iron.

7 Stuff the warmed pita bread with the lamb, tomato, onion, and tzatziki sauce. Serve with more sauce on the side.

Waffled Croque Madame

| **IRON:** Belgian or standard | **TIME:** 5 hours with brioche dough from scratch (30 minutes with store-bought crescent dough) | **YIELD:** Serves up to 6 |

Once you get the hang of waffling an egg, you won't be able to resist the wow factor.

Sandra Holl owns and runs Floriole Cafe & Bakery with her husband, Mathieu, on Chicago's North Side. This recipe was her brainstorm. We worked out the details first in a cramped kitchen before her bakery debuted and then in her beautiful, sunlit bakery kitchen a few years later.

Ordinarily, I wouldn't get your hopes up, because I live my life by the motto that people with low expectations are rarely disappointed. But I'm just going to say: You have a winner on your hands here.

It does take a bit of work, though.

The crowning glory of this recipe is the waffled egg. Waffling an egg requires two things in abundance: butter and patience. A silicone spatula goes a long way, too.

Both Brioche Dough and crescent dough are possibilities as a base for the Croque Madame.

If you want to do this the long way from scratch, the recipe for Brioche Dough follows. Otherwise, crescent dough is available in the supermarket's refrigerated case. If you're using store-bought

dough, make the Béchamel Sauce first and then proceed with cooking and assembling the Croque Madame. If you're making the Brioche Dough from scratch, make the Béchamel Sauce when the dough has 20 minutes left in its final rise.

The layers of waffling—the waffled egg atop the waffled cheese resting on a base of waffled dough—make this impressive at a glance. Tastewise, the waffled texture of the base allows the Béchamel Sauce to pool in the divots.

It works on every level.

1 Preheat the waffle iron on medium.

2 IF YOU'RE USING CRESCENT DOUGH: The dough will likely come out of the tube in a wedge shape, but it can be assembled into a square. Cut the wedge of dough in half to make two triangles. Shape the triangles into a square 4 to 5 inches on each side and press the edges together gently. Using a silicone brush, coat both sides of one section of the waffle iron with the melted butter, place the dough on that section of the waffle iron, close the lid, and cook the dough until it is golden brown, about 3 minutes. Remove the dough from the waffle iron and transfer to a cutting board or plate.

IF YOU'RE USING BRIOCHE DOUGH: Using a silicone brush, coat both sides of one section of the waffle iron with the melted butter and cook the dough on one section of the waffle iron with the lid closed until the dough is golden brown, about 4 minutes. Remove the dough from the waffle iron and transfer to a cutting board or plate.

3 Pour the Béchamel Sauce onto the waffled dough. (The sauce will mostly pool in the divots.) Then layer the ham on top. Sprinkle the shredded cheese on top. Place the assembled stack in the waffle iron and close the lid for 10 seconds to melt the cheese and marry the layers. Remove the stack from the waffle iron.

4 Crack an egg into a small cup or ramekin. This will give you control over how the egg lands on the waffle iron. Brush the remaining melted butter on the lower grid of one section of the waffle iron and pour the egg onto that section. Cook, without closing the lid, until the white

For 1 Croque Madame:

1 piece crescent dough (from a tube of prepared crescent rolls) or Brioche Dough (recipe follows)

1 tablespoon unsalted butter, melted

3 tablespoons Béchamel Sauce (recipe follows)

2 slices Black Forest ham

¼ cup shredded Gruyère cheese

1 large egg

NOTE: Brioche and béchamel recipes make 6 servings; servings with store-bought crescent dough may vary.

has set, about 1 minute, and continue cooking until the yolk has set a bit, 1 or 2 minutes. To remove the egg intact, use an offset spatula or a pair of heat-resistant silicone spatulas to coax it from the grid of the waffle iron. Loosen the edges first, and then lift out the egg while supporting it from below as much as possible.

5 Top the sandwich with the egg and serve hot.

INGREDIENTS

1 cup milk

2 tablespoons unsalted butter

2 tablespoons flour

¼ teaspoon salt

Freshly ground black pepper, to taste

Pinch of grated nutmeg

Béchamel Sauce

1 Bring the milk to room temperature in a small saucepan over low heat, or in the microwave for 45 seconds.

2 Melt the butter in a small saucepan over medium-low heat. Add the flour to the melted butter, whisking constantly until it darkens slightly, 2 minutes.

3 Whisk in the milk in 2 batches, waiting until the mixture is thoroughly combined before adding the second half. Whisk constantly over medium-low heat until the mixture thickens to the consistency of thick cream, about 5 minutes. Add the salt and a pinch each of pepper and nutmeg, then taste to check the seasoning.

Brioche Dough

1   Place the 2 cups flour, yeast, salt, and sugar in a food processor and pulse to combine.

2   Add the 4 tablespoons butter and eggs and pulse 10 times until well combined. Add the milk and process until the ingredients come together, 30 seconds. The mixture will be very sticky—the texture should be somewhere between a batter and a dough.

3   Lightly grease a large bowl with butter and place the mixture in it. Cover with plastic wrap or a damp towel, and let rise in a warm place until the dough has doubled in size, 3 hours.

4   Scrape the dough onto a lightly floured surface, dust the top with flour, and use well-floured hands to shape it into a rough rectangle, about 6 inches wide and 9 inches long. Cut once down the length of the dough (don't saw) to leave 2 sections about 3 inches by 9 inches. Cut each section into 3 equal parts, to make 6 squares about 3 inches on each side. Pat down the squares and stretch them slightly so that they're about 5 inches on each side. Cover them with a damp towel and let rise in a warm place for an hour, or until they are slightly puffy.

5   After an hour, the dough can be used or frozen by wrapping in plastic and storing in a zip-top bag. Let frozen dough come to room temperature before using.

INGREDIENTS

2 cups all-purpose flour, plus more for dusting

1 teaspoon instant yeast

½ teaspoon salt

2 tablespoons granulated sugar

4 tablespoons cold unsalted butter, cut into 8 pieces, plus more for greasing the bowl

2 large eggs

½ cup milk

Classic Waffleburger
with Cheese

IRON: Belgian or standard | **TIME:** 20 minutes with store-bought buns | **YIELD:** Serves 4

An all-time favorite classic meets the waffle iron and is transformed.

NOTE: Buns made from scratch will take about four hours due to the dough's rising time.

Waffleburgers are the best marriage of whimsy and familiarity. Now, you can do this the easy way or the hard way. You can just waffle some hamburger meat, slap it between two buns from a bag, and call it a day. Easy.

But you could just as easily cook your hamburger in a frying pan like a normal person. And that's not exactly why we're here.

So to take this dish to its logical, waffled conclusion, there's a recipe for making your own buns in the waffle iron—giving you a truly waffled burger from start to finish.

Of course, life gets in the way. You're not always—or ever?—going to have time to make your buns from scratch. So I won't blame you if you take the easy route, as long as you heat the store-bought buns in the waffle iron. Put them in the waffle iron for about 10 seconds—on medium, with the lid closed, to get grid marks on both sides—and then keep them warm in a low oven until the patties are ready.

INGREDIENTS

Nonstick cooking spray

1 pound ground beef

½ teaspoon salt

1 teaspoon freshly ground
    black pepper

4 slices American, Cheddar,
    or Gruyère cheese
    (optional)

4 store-bought or
    homemade hamburger
    buns

Ketchup, mustard, lettuce,
    tomato, and pickles,
    for serving

NOTE: To make homemade buns, follow the subrecipe for Brioche Dough on page 53, substituting an equal amount of buttermilk for the milk. Using buttermilk helps develop a tender crumb and gives the buns a bit of a sourdough-like tang. When you're ready to cook the buns, preheat the waffle iron on medium and brush the grid with the melted butter. Brush the flour off one square of dough, place it on the waffle iron, close the lid, and cook until light golden brown, 3 minutes.

1 Preheat the waffle iron on medium. Coat both sides of the waffle iron grid with nonstick spray.

2 Season the beef with the salt and pepper and form it into 4 patties, each roughly the shape of the buns.

3 Place as many patties as will fit in the waffle iron, close the lid, and cook until the beef reaches an internal temperature of 160°F on an instant-read thermometer, 3 minutes.

4 When the patties have cooked, remove them from the waffle iron. If you would like a waffleburger with cheese, leave a patty in the waffle iron, top with the cheese, and close the lid to waffle very briefly—about 5 seconds.

5 Repeat Steps 3 and 4 with any remaining patties.

6 Serve on a bun with ketchup, mustard, lettuce, tomato, and pickles.

Waffled Portobello Mushroom with Italian Herbs

IRON: Belgian or Standard | **TIME:** 40 minutes, including 30 minutes marinating | **YIELD:** Serves 1

Serve the mushrooms whole as a main course, or cut them into strips to serve as a side dish.

I love the idea of a four-ingredient recipe that turns into a satisfying, impressive meal. Okay, fine. I didn't count salt and pepper. Six ingredients, then.

Did I mention it's vegetarian? It's vegetarian—vegan, even—but not for the sake of being vegetarian or vegan. It just happens to be delicious that way. If you'd like, you can melt some cheese atop the finished product. For a full meal, serve it with a simple salad and some polenta.

1 In a shallow bowl or deep dish, combine the oils, herbs, salt, and pepper. Stir to evenly distribute the herbs.

2 To prepare the mushrooms, scoop out the gills with a spoon and wipe down the mushroom cap with a damp paper towel to remove any dirt.

3 Place the mushroom caps in the oil mixture and marinate for at least 30 minutes, turning them over about halfway through.

INGREDIENTS

¼ cup extra-virgin olive oil

¼ cup neutral-flavored oil, such as canola

1 tablespoon Italian herbs (or 1 teaspoon each dried rosemary, dried basil, and dried oregano)

¼ teaspoon salt

¼ teaspoon freshly ground black pepper

2 portobello mushrooms, stems snapped off and discarded

4 Preheat the waffle iron on medium.

5 Place the mushrooms, cap side up, in the waffle iron and close the lid.

6 Check the mushrooms after 5 minutes. The caps should be soft and cooked through. Remove the mushrooms from the waffle iron and serve.

VARIATION

Top with melted cheese: When the mushrooms have cooked for 5 minutes, lift the lid, place slices of mozzarella or fontina atop the mushrooms, and close the lid for 20 seconds.

If the cheese has not melted sufficiently, continue cooking with the lid down for another 10 seconds. A little cheese may be left behind on the grid. This is for the cook.

TIPS

• Prepare the recipe through Step 3 and allow the mushrooms to marinate overnight in the refrigerator. The next day, you'll have a meal ready in about 5 minutes.

• Serve as a sandwich on a toasted bun with blue cheese and caramelized onions.

Waffled Filet Mignon

IRON: Belgian or standard | **TIME:** 15 minutes | **YIELD:** Serves 2

With steak, your first instinct may not be to reach for the waffle iron. This recipe should fix that.

People are going to think you're nuts when you throw an expensive piece of meat—one synonymous with luxury—in the waffle iron. They won't think you're nuts when they eat it. (Or at least they'll forget momentarily.) The outside develops a spectacular char. The inside stays silky smooth. The waffle marks? Those are just a bonus.

Some recipes recommend aggressive sauces for filet mignon, arguing that the texture is impeccable but the flavor leaves something to be desired. Me, I find a simple salt and pepper crust to be best. Add a salad of tomatoes and blue cheese with a balsamic vinaigrette drizzle, and you have an equation for the perfect meal.

With steak, timing is everything. This is where your instant-read digital thermometer really comes in handy. After 9 minutes in the waffle iron, my first filet was barely cracking 110°F. I let it go another 3 minutes. By the time I checked again, it was 165°F at its coolest part. In other words, the temperature snowballed as time went on. That first steak was delicious, but more done than I would have liked.

The second steak was much improved. After 10 minutes, I checked and found it was at 130°F—quite rare. I let it go another 90 seconds and checked again. It was 140°F—on the rare side of medium. Perfect for my purposes. I removed it and let it rest for 5 minutes.

One final word of advice: Err on the side of undercooking and then correct with another 1 or 2 minutes in the waffle iron, if necessary.

INGREDIENTS

2 teaspoons coarse sea salt
   or kosher salt

2 teaspoons freshly ground
   black pepper

8 ounces filet mignon,
   about 1½ inches thick

Nonstick cooking spray

NOTE: Cooking times
will vary according to the
thickness of the steak and
your waffle iron. If your
steak is thinner or thicker
than 1½ inches, you'll
want to check on it 1 or 2
minutes earlier or later
than the times indicated.

1 Preheat the waffle iron on high.

2 Pour the salt and pepper onto a plate, mix to distribute evenly, and coat the steak with the mixture on both sides.

3 Coat both sides of the waffle iron grid with nonstick spray. Put the steak on the waffle iron as far away from the hinge as possible. (This allows for the lid to press down on the meat more evenly.) Close the lid and cook for 8 minutes.

4 If you have an instant-read thermometer, check the temperature of the steak after 8 minutes. For a steak cooked medium, the temperature should read 140°F. (A temperature of 130°F will give you a medium-rare steak; 155°F is well done.) If it needs to cook further,
check about every minute and remove when it has reached your desired temperature. If you do not have an instant-read thermometer, check after 8 minutes, making an incision in the top of the steak about ¾ inch deep. When the steak is ready to remove, you should see only a bit of pink toward its center.

5 Remove the steak and place it on a cutting board. Leave the waffle iron on, in case you need to cook the steak a bit more.

6 Allow the steak to rest for several minutes before slicing it in half and checking doneness. If it's done to your satisfaction, turn off the waffle iron and serve. If you'd like it less rare, return it to the waffle iron and check after another minute. Let the steak rest once more before serving.

Spaghetti and Waffled Meatballs

IRON: Belgian or standard | **TIME:** 90 minutes | **YIELD:** Serves 4

waffling the meatballs creates little pockets that collect the sauce beautifully.

"Can I borrow your family?"

That was me talking.

My dear friends Nick and Anya have two adorable young children. I have none. (It's not that my children are ugly; I don't have any.) But, I had a hunch that waffling meatballs would be popular among the younger set. To confirm this, I needed a family.

Our schedules were crazy, and in the end it made more sense for me to come to them. Before I left my house, I asked them the question I've trained myself to ask in these situations: "Do you have a waffle iron?"

They did. A beautiful one. Snatched up at a yard sale, it was probably older than anyone in the room. It had the soft lines of a classic car. This thing had seen some waffles.

It was about to see some meatballs.

Nick made a salad while I assembled the meatballs.

When it came time for the meat to hit the grid, the oldest boy was called into the room. "He's going to want to see this," Nick said.

Perched on a stepladder, the boy watched as the meatballs went into the waffle iron and the lid was closed.

"What are they called?" he asked the room. "Are they meatwaffles or waffleballs?"

Wow. This kid got right to it.

When the meatballs came out, he pointed to the one he wanted. I promised I would mark it with his initials. And I did, carefully. Couldn't have him sending his plate back to the kitchen.

To make this all come together, begin preparing the sauce first, so it can simmer, and let the water come to a boil while you work on the meatballs. Then you can cook the meatballs and the pasta at the same time. (Or cook the meatballs first and keep them warm in the preheated oven while you cook the pasta.)

1 Make the marinara sauce: Cut each clove of garlic in half and flatten it with the flat side of a knife blade, pressing down with your palm to crush the garlic. Remove the garlic peel. (It should come off easily.)

2 Place the 2 tablespoons of olive oil and the crushed garlic cloves in a large saucepan over medium-low heat. Cook until the garlic is fragrant and just beginning to turn golden, about 3 minutes.

3 While the garlic is cooking, partially drain the tomatoes by pouring off only the liquid at the top of the can. Use a fork or kitchen shears to rip the tomatoes into large, uneven chunks in the can.

4 Add the tomatoes and red pepper flakes to the saucepan, taking care to guard against splashing as the tomatoes meet the hot oil.

5 Cook over medium heat until the sauce begins to bubble, about 5 minutes. Simmer on medium-low heat, stirring occasionally, until the tomatoes break down, 45 minutes. You should be left with a thick, somewhat chunky sauce. Taste and adjust the seasoning by adding salt and pepper.

6 Make the pasta: Bring a large pot of water to a boil over high heat.

7 Preheat the waffle iron on medium. Preheat the oven on its lowest setting.

INGREDIENTS

Marinara sauce and pasta:

4 cloves garlic, unpeeled

2 tablespoons extra-virgin olive oil, plus more for serving

2 cans (28 ounces each) whole plum tomatoes

¼ teaspoon red pepper flakes

Salt and freshly ground black pepper, to taste

12 ounces spaghetti

Waffled meatballs:

1 pound lean ground beef or turkey

10 ounces frozen chopped spinach, thawed and squeezed dry

1 large egg, lightly beaten

¼ cup plain bread crumbs

¼ cup finely chopped onion

¼ cup grated Parmesan cheese, plus more for serving

2 cloves garlic, minced

½ teaspoon salt

Nonstick cooking spray

Freshly grated Parmesan, or other hard cheese, for serving

8 While the sauce simmers and the pasta water comes to a boil, make the meatballs: In a large mixing bowl, combine all of the ingredients for the meatballs, except for the cooking spray, and mix well.

9 Form the mixture into 16 balls and place on a cutting board covered with waxed or parchment paper.

10 Add the spaghetti to the boiling water and cook according to package directions. Drain and keep warm.

11 Coat both sides of the waffle iron grid with nonstick spray. Place as many meatballs as will fit on the waffle iron, leaving a bit of space for each to expand when flattened.

12 Close the lid and cook until the meatballs are browned on the outside and cooked through, 6 minutes. You may have to cut into one to make sure that no traces of pink remain. If you have an instant-read thermometer, beef should be at least 160°F and turkey should be at least 165°F.

13 Remove the meatballs from the waffle iron. Repeat Steps 11 and 12 to cook the remaining meatballs. If the other components are not ready yet, keep the meatballs warm in the preheated oven.

14 Serve a generous portion of pasta with 4 waffled meatballs, topped sparingly with sauce. Drizzle with extra-virgin olive oil and dust with Parmesan. Serve extra sauce at the table.

Waffled Macaroni and Cheese

IRON: Belgian or standard	**TIME:** 4½ hours (includes preparation of macaroni and cheese, plus 3 hours of refrigeration time)	**YIELD:** Serves 8

Leftover mac and cheese is not exactly one of life's biggest problems, but if it happens to you, here's what to do.

This isn't so much about how to *make* macaroni and cheese as it is about what to do with leftovers. So while you may find your own path to macaroni and cheese, I have included my favorite recipe. If you have no leftovers (completely understandable) and you make the macaroni and cheese specifically for this purpose, that's fine too, of course. But you're going to have to let it cool in the refrigerator for a while. It needs to be easy to handle.

There were a lot of false starts on waffling macaroni and cheese. At first, I tried just waffling the cooked and cooled chunks, but after a few minutes in the waffle iron, the cheese had melted away and the macaroni stubbornly refused to conform to the grid of the waffle iron. It had all of the easily imaginable drawbacks of waffled macaroni and cheese—cheese melts easily, after all—and none of the advantages (that is, no discernible waffle form).

Then I decided to get clever, which, as you may suspect, didn't lead to anything good.

If the noodles were refusing to bend to the will and the weight of the waffle iron, I thought maybe I could cut them down to size. So I dumped a batch of cold macaroni and cheese into the food processor and gave it a whirl. I envisioned the resulting pellet-size bits of macaroni and cheese conforming easily to the grids of the waffle iron, fusing together into one magnificent macaroni and cheese waffle.

Not so much.

So what did work? Breading it.

The bread crumbs come between the intense heat of the waffle iron and the cheese and allow the whole thing to stay intact—just barely. It takes a light touch. You should be prepared for some things to fall apart.

Three notes about making the macaroni and cheese itself:

First, when making the sauce, use a saucepan large enough to accommodate the pasta, because you'll end up pouring the pasta into the sauce in the end.

Also, if the milk, butter, and flour mixture doesn't thicken after 5 minutes or so, you're better off starting that part over with new butter and flour rather than throwing all the cheese in there and hoping for the best. The best won't happen; you'll just end up with gloppy macaroni and cheese.

And, lastly, if you use a small, regular shape like elbows, the recipe will fit perfectly in a 9 by 5-inch loaf pan. If you use a more exotic shape, you might have a bit of overflow, which of course you will be obligated to eat while the macaroni and cheese bakes in the pan.

Hey, no one said this would be easy.

INGREDIENTS

Prepared Macaroni and Cheese (recipe follows)

2 large eggs

Pinch each of salt and freshly ground black pepper

1 cup all-purpose flour

1 cup seasoned bread crumbs

1/4 cup grated hard cheese, such as Parmesan or Pecorino Romano

Nonstick cooking spray

1 Cut the macaroni and cheese into slices about 1/2 inch thick.

2 Preheat the waffle iron on medium. Preheat the oven on its lowest setting.

3 In a small bowl, beat the egg with a pinch each of salt and pepper.

4 Set out 3 shallow bowls. Measure the flour into the first. In the second bowl, place the beaten eggs. Mix the bread crumbs with the cheese in the third.

5 Take a slice of the macaroni and cheese, and, handling it

TIP

Serve with a green salad or Crispy Sesame Waffled Kale (see page 128).

gently, coat both sides in the flour. Then dunk both sides in the egg. Finally, coat both sides with the bread crumbs, pressing the mixture so it sticks. Set aside the slice and repeat with the remaining slices.

6   Coat both sides of the waffle iron grid with nonstick spray. Place the macaroni and cheese slices in the waffle iron, close the lid, and cook until heated through and golden brown, 3 minutes.

7   The extraction process can be tricky. With a silicone spatula, loosen the edges of the macaroni and cheese. Use the spatula to gently pry the macaroni and cheese from the waffle iron and then support the bottom with the spatula while you lift it out with tongs.

8   Repeat Steps 5 through 7 until all of the macaroni and cheese has been waffled. Keep the finished macaroni and cheese warm in the oven.

INGREDIENTS

3 tablespoons unsalted butter, plus more for greasing pan

Salt

1 pound elbow or shell pasta

3 tablespoons all-purpose flour

1½ cups milk

½ teaspoon yellow or Dijon mustard

¼ teaspoon freshly ground black pepper

2 cups shredded extra-sharp Cheddar cheese

½ cup grated Parmesan cheese

Macaroni and Cheese

I   Preheat the oven to 375°F. Butter a 9 x 5-inch loaf pan and set it aside.

2   Bring a large pot of salted water to a boil over high heat. When the water is at a rolling boil, add the pasta. Cook the pasta until it is slightly underdone, checking a few minutes before the cooking time on the package directions. (If you bite into a piece, you should be able to see a very thin core of uncooked pasta.) Drain the pasta and set aside.

3   Melt the 3 tablespoons butter in a large saucepan over medium-low heat. Add the flour to the melted butter, whisking constantly. Continue to whisk for 2 minutes. Add the milk, ½ cup at a time, waiting until the mixture is thoroughly combined before adding more. Whisk constantly over medium-low heat until the mixture thickens to the consistency of heavy cream, about 5 minutes.

4   Turn off the heat, add the mustard, 1¼ teaspoon salt, and pepper, and stir. Add the shredded Cheddar cheese a handful at a time, stirring constantly until the cheese melts. Add the pasta to the cheese mixture, stir to coat thoroughly, and then pour the cheese-covered pasta into the prepared loaf pan.

5 Sprinkle the grated Parmesan cheese on top and bake until the top is brown and crispy, about 20 minutes.

6 Set aside to cool for an hour, then cover with plastic wrap and refrigerate until the macaroni is well chilled and the cheese has solidified (at least 2 hours, or overnight).

Toasted Cheese Wavioli

IRON: Standard (ravioli cooked in a Belgian-style machine won't bear many waffle marks because they are too small)	**TIME:** 25 minutes	**YIELD:** Serves 2

In which the waffle iron stands in for a deep fryer.

Toasted ravioli are a tradition in St. Louis, where they're typically deep-fried. If you grab a package of ravioli from the supermarket, you can have this meal on the table in less than 30 minutes—without the hassle of deep-frying.

I struggled with striking the right balance for this recipe. At first, the ravioli were taking too long to cook. By the time they were browned and crispy, the filling was dry. But removing them from the waffle iron too soon meant the coating was pale and limp.

Then my mom stepped in: Why not add olive oil to the coating mix? The oil helps the coating brown more quickly, so the ravioli come out golden brown without being too dry. Success. (Thanks, Mom.)

½ cup milk

1 large egg

1 tablespoon extra-virgin olive oil

1 cup seasoned bread crumbs

½ teaspoon salt

½ teaspoon garlic powder

½ pound cheese ravioli, chilled

Nonstick cooking spray

1 cup marinara sauce (see Spaghetti and Waffled Meatballs, Steps 1 to 5, page 65)

1 Preheat the waffle iron on medium. Cover a baking sheet with wax or parchment paper and set it aside. Preheat the oven on its lowest setting.

2 In a small bowl, whisk together the milk, egg, and olive oil.

3 In another small bowl, combine the bread crumbs, salt, and garlic powder.

4 Dip the ravioli first into the milk mixture, coating both sides, then dip in the bread crumb mixture, pressing the mixture so it sticks. Place the coated ravioli on the prepared baking sheet.

5 Coat both sides of the waffle iron grid with nonstick spray. Heat the marinara sauce in a small saucepan over medium heat or in the microwave for 1 minute.

6 Place as many ravioli as will fit in the waffle iron, close the lid, and cook for 2 minutes, or until crispy and toasted.

7 Remove the ravioli from the waffle iron and repeat Step 6 with the remaining ravioli. Keep the finished ravioli warm in the oven.

8 Serve with the marinara sauce for dipping.

Waffled Sweet Potato Gnocchi

IRON: Standard preferred | **TIME:** 2 hours | **YIELD:** Serves 4 (makes about 60 gnocchi)

These could easily become your new once-a-month tradition.

NOTE: A Belgian iron can be used for the boiling method (see page 77), but your gnocchi won't bear many waffle marks if they are cooked entirely in a Belgian iron.

Living in Argentina gave me an appreciation for gnocchi. Although Europe is an ocean away, immigration left its mark and Italian influence is strong there. The 29th of every month was gnocchi day. Lines formed at pasta shops to buy gnocchi for the evening meal.

Why gnocchi and why on that day? The idea is that it's the end of the month and the pantry is bare. The ingredients for gnocchi couldn't be more humble: potatoes and flour, though many people add some Parmesan and maybe an egg. Maybe you don't have much, but you have enough to make gnocchi. And gnocchi are comforting and filling.

Gnocchi often get lumped in the pasta section of the menu, but in truth they are potato dumplings. Many recipes use boiled potatoes, but this recipe uses baked. The fluffy, dry texture of the baked potato means we can control the amount of moisture added, in the form of an egg.

If you're serious about gnocchi, you use a ridged paddle called a gnocchi board to put the trademark indentations in the gnocchi. If you're not serious about gnocchi—or have a healthy disregard for tradition—you use a waffle iron.

INGREDIENTS

1 large baking potato
   (such as russet) and
   1 large sweet potato
   (about 1½ pounds total)

1¼ cups all-purpose flour,
   plus more for flouring the
   work surface

½ cup grated Parmesan
   cheese

1 teaspoon salt

½ teaspoon freshly ground
   black pepper

Dash of grated nutmeg
   (optional)

1 large egg, beaten

Nonstick cooking spray or
   melted buter

Pesto or Waffled Sage
   and Butter Sauce
   (recipes follow)

There are two cooking methods. The first method is cooking the gnocchi to completion in the waffle iron. This results in golden brown dumplings that pair nicely with a pesto sauce.

The second method is the surprise: You don't even turn on the waffle iron. Use the waffle iron grid to shape the dough and then cook the gnocchi in boiling water. This gives you waffled dumplings that are moist and pillowy, and the gnocchi's indentations hold the sauce of your choosing beautifully.

I Preheat the oven to 350°F.

2 Bake the potatoes until easily pierced with a fork, about an hour. Let the potatoes cool slightly, then peel them. (They may be just shy of the texture you'd want in a baked potato, but keep in mind they're being cooked again later.) Pass the potatoes through a food mill or a ricer or grate them over the large holes of a box grater and into a large bowl.

3 Add the 1¼ cups flour to the potatoes and use your hands to mix them together, breaking up any lumps of potato along the way. Sprinkle the cheese, salt, pepper, and nutmeg over the dough and knead lightly to distribute evenly.

4 Once the flour and potatoes are combined, make a well in the center of the bowl and add the beaten egg. Using your fingers, work the egg through the dough

until it starts to come together. It will be slightly sticky.

5 On a lightly floured surface, gently knead the dough a few times to bring it together. It should be moist, but not wet and sticky. If it's too sticky, add 1 tablespoon flour at a time, up to ¼ cup. Roll the dough into a log and cut it into 4 pieces.

6 Roll each piece into a rope about the diameter of your thumb and then use a sharp knife to cut into 1-inch segments.

7 Preheat the waffle iron on medium. Coat both sides of the waffle iron grid with nonstick spray, or butter the grids using a silicone pastry brush. Turn down the oven to its lowest setting and set aside a baking sheet to keep the finished gnocchi warm.

8 Gently shake off any residual flour from the gnocchi and place a batch on the waffle iron, leaving a bit of space for

each to expand. Close the lid and cook until the grid marks on the gnocchi are golden brown, 2 minutes. Repeat with the remaining gnocchi, keeping the cooked gnocchi warm on the baking sheet in the oven.

9 Serve hot with Pesto Sauce or Waffled Sage and Butter Sauce.

VARIATION

There's another method possible: shaping the gnocchi in the waffle iron and boiling them.

Follow the recipe through Step 6. Do not turn on the waffle iron. Dust the gnocchi lightly with flour, place them in the waffle iron, leaving space for the gnocchi to spread a bit, and close the lid. After 10 seconds, lift the lid, remove the gnocchi, and set them aside on a plate. Repeat until you've shaped all the gnocchi. At this point, the gnocchi can be boiled until they float, about 2 minutes, or flash-frozen in a single layer on a baking sheet for an hour, and then transferred to a zip-top bag for storage in the freezer. Frozen gnocchi will take an extra minute to cook.

NOTE: If you're shaping in a Belgian-style waffle iron, you'll have to carefully place the gnocchi directly on the raised waffle grid to get the right shape.

Pesto Sauce

TIME: 10 minutes | **YIELD:** Makes 1 cup

Combine the basil, garlic, nuts, olive oil, and cheese in a food processor. Pulse until well mixed. Extra pesto can be stored in a covered container in the refrigerator for several days. (The color of the pesto may darken; it's still delicious.) Or freeze the pesto in ice cube trays then move the frozen cubes to a zip-top bag.

INGREDIENTS

2 cups fresh basil leaves, washed and well dried

1 small clove garlic

3 tablespoons pine nuts or walnuts

½ cup extra-virgin olive oil

½ cup grated Parmesan cheese

4 tablespoons (½ stick)
salted butter, melted

16 large fresh sage leaves

Waffled Sage and Butter Sauce

TIME: 5 minutes | **YIELD:** Makes ¼ cup

I Preheat the waffle iron on medium.

2 Dip the sage leaves in melted butter and place them in the waffle iron until they are crispy and slightly browned, I minute.

3 Pour the melted butter over the gnocchi and garnish with waffled sage leaves.

Pressed Potato and Cheese Pierogi

IRON: Belgian or standard | **TIME:** 2 hours | **YIELD:** Serves 4

Serve these with sautéed onions, sour cream, and applesauce.

Potato and cheese pierogi are unapologetically Old World, laden with fat and carbohydrates. Slathered with butter, or served piping hot with sour cream, they are the ultimate comfort food for a cold night.

INGREDIENTS

Dough:

2¼ cups all-purpose flour, plus more for dusting the work surface as needed

½ teaspoon salt

2 large eggs

⅓ cup water, or more as needed

Filling:

1 pound russet (baking) potatoes, peeled and cut into 1-inch cubes

½ cup shredded Cheddar cheese

2 tablespoons unsalted butter

1 teaspoon salt

1 teaspoon freshly ground black pepper

Nonstick cooking spray

The trick to making them in the waffle iron is to get the dough nice and thin. Pierogi dough expands a bit when cooked, so a thick slab becomes something you gnaw instead of chew. The key is to first press the dough with your hand to flatten it and then use a rolling pin to get it uniformly thin. The thinner dough also makes for bigger pierogi . . . meaning, you can stuff more filling in there. Even so, this recipe may leave you with extra filling, but it's better to have too much than to end up short. Any extra can be stored in the refrigerator. (Reheat it and stir in a bit of milk or cream to serve it as a side dish.)

Be smart about how you assemble the pierogi by doing a few at a time, assembly-line style. First pat out several pieces of dough, then roll them out thin, then fill them before crimping them and starting from the beginning with another round of dough.

1 Make the dough: In a large bowl, combine the 2¼ cups flour and salt.

2 In a small bowl, beat the eggs and the ⅓ cup water together. Add the eggs to the flour mixture and mix the dough with a wooden spoon or your hands until it can be shaped into a ball. If the dough needs more water to come together, add 1 tablespoon of water at a time until the dough just holds together but is not sticky. If the dough is too sticky (unlikely, but possible), add 1 tablespoon of flour at a time.

3 Wrap the ball of dough in plastic wrap and set it in the refrigerator for 30 minutes.

4 Meanwhile, make the filling: Place the potatoes in a medium-size pot, cover them with cold water, and bring to a boil, covered, over medium-high heat. Once the water is boiling, remove the cover and simmer the potatoes over low heat until they are soft and easily pierced with a knife, about 10 minutes. Drain the potatoes in a colander.

5 Transfer the potatoes to a large bowl, and mash them together with the shredded cheese, butter, salt, and pepper. Allow the mixture to cool to room temperature.

6 Generously dust a work surface with flour and shape the chilled dough into a roll about

24 inches long. (The width does not matter as long as it's fairly uniform.) Cut the dough into 24 equal portions and form a ball out of each portion of dough.

7 Flatten a dough ball with your hand. With a rolling pin, roll the dough into a rough circle and make it as thin as you can while keeping it easy to handle. Place a heaping teaspoon of the filling in the center, leaving a border of no more than ½ inch. Fold the pierogi in half and crimp the edges with a fork. Set the finished pierogi on a floured surface, cover with plastic wrap or a clean lint-free towel, and repeat with the rest of the dough and filling.

8 Preheat the waffle iron on medium. Preheat the oven on its lowest setting.

9 Coat both sides of the waffle iron grid with nonstick spray, place as many pierogi as will fit in the waffle iron, and close the lid.

10 Waffle until the dough is cooked and the pierogi are light golden brown, 3 minutes. Remove the cooked pierogi.

11 Repeat Steps 9 and 10 until all pierogi have been waffled. Keep finished pierogi warm in the oven.

VARIATIONS

Add one of the following to the potato filling in Step 5:

- ¼ teaspoon cayenne pepper
- ¼ teaspoon paprika
- ½ teaspoon ground cumin
- 1 teaspoon minced garlic
- ¼ teaspoon dry mustard

Pizza Margherita
with Waffled Crust

| **IRON:** Belgian or standard | **TIME:** 3½ hours (including time for dough to rise) | **YIELD:** Serves 6 |

This one came together with the help of a pizza expert.

Dimitri Syrkin-Nikolau opened the doors, and the pizza ovens, of Dimo's Pizza on Chicago's North Side—and really went to town. We tested some pretty outrageous waffled pizzas: mashed potato, stuffing, and gravy pizza; chicken, waffles, and crème fraîche pizza; and crab, cream cheese, and sweet-and-sour sauce pizza. Most important, we learned what works and what doesn't.

There are two ways to go here: the more traditional pizza-like waffled pizza, where the toppings sit atop the crust, and the calzone-style waffled pizza, where the dough encases the filling. The first method marries waffle and pizza with minimum fuss: Cook the dough in the waffle iron and then fudge it ever so slightly—really, it's not cheating because I've done this myself and what am I if not the arbiter of all things waffled?—and stick it under the broiler to finish. Voilà. Pizza on a waffled crust.

If you can get the dough thin enough, the calzone-style waffled pizza has something to offer; it's certainly the version that looks most like a waffle. And you don't have to heat up the oven. The only possible drawback with doing it this way is the tendency for the result to be too bready. After all, it's going to have two crusts.

INGREDIENTS

Crust:

4 cups bread flour, plus more for dusting

1 teaspoon instant yeast

1½ teaspoons salt

1½ cups lukewarm water

Neutral-flavored oil, such as canola, for coating the bowl

Nonstick cooking spray

Topping:

3 cups marinara sauce (see Tips, opposite)

2 cups shredded mozzarella

1 pint cherry tomatoes, halved (optional)

1 large bunch basil, washed, dried, and finely chopped

1 Make the crust: In a large bowl, combine the flour, yeast, and salt. Add the water and mix until the dough is shaggy and most of the water has been absorbed. Turn the dough out of the bowl onto a lightly floured counter and knead until it is just blended but not too smooth. Cover the dough with a damp towel or plastic wrap and let it rest for 10 to 15 minutes.

2 Knead the dough until it is fairly smooth, 5 to 10 minutes.

3 Coat a bowl with the oil, add the dough to the bowl, and turn to coat. Let the dough rise in a warm place, covered with plastic wrap, for 2½ hours, or until nearly doubled in size.

4 Dust your work surface with more flour. Punch down the dough, divide it into 6 pieces, place the pieces on your work surface, and form each into a smooth ball. Allow the pieces to rest for 5 minutes, covered by a cloth or plastic wrap. When you are ready to waffle, remove the wrap and shape each piece into a disk, pulling gradually on the dough to expand it. If it resists, let it rest for 5 minutes before continuing.

5 Preheat the waffle iron on medium. Coat both sides of the waffle iron grid with nonstick spray.

6 Pull a disk of dough evenly until it's as thin as possible, roughly circular, and about 8 inches in diameter (but no bigger than your waffle iron). If the dough tears, repair the tear by pushing the dough together and continuing to stretch other parts of the dough. Repeat with each dough disk.

7 Preheat the broiler.

8 Put a disk of dough in the waffle iron and cook about 5 minutes, or until golden brown.

9 Remove the disk from the waffle iron and set it on a baking sheet. Repeat Step 8 with the remaining disks.

10 Top each waffled crust with about ½ cup of sauce, ⅓ cup of cheese, and a handful of the tomatoes, if using, and place the baking sheet under the broiler for about 2 minutes, until the cheese is melted and bubbling.

11 Remove the pizzas from the broiler, sprinkle with basil, and serve warm.

VARIATION

Interested in a version that is waffled from start to finish? I give you the Waffled Calzone:

1 After the disks have been formed in Step 6, put ¼ cup of sauce, ¼ cup of cheese, a few tomatoes, if using, and a small handful of basil on one half of the dough, leaving a margin of about ½ inch all around. Fold over the dough to envelop the toppings in a pocket and pinch the edges to seal. Place the pocket in the waffle iron and close the lid.

2 Cook for 5 minutes and then check. The cooking time will depend on the thickness of the dough. Calzones with very thin dough may be done after 5 minutes. Thicker dough may take a few more minutes. The dough should be golden brown and the cheese should be melted.

3 Repeat with the remaining ingredients. Serve warm with extra marinara sauce for dipping.

TIPS

- This recipe makes more dough than you're likely to use at one time. That's definitely an advantage, not a disadvantage. Put any extra dough in an oiled zip-top bag. Pizza dough will store beautifully in the freezer for months. Just let it come to room temperature in a bowl covered with plastic wrap before you proceed.

- For the marinara sauce, you can use a store-bought version, or make the recipe from the Spaghetti and Waffled Meatballs (Steps 1 to 5, page 65) cooked down for an additional hour.

Chicken Parmesan
with Waffled Vegetables

IRON: Belgian or standard | **TIME:** 30 minutes | **YIELD:** Serves 4

A dash of hot sauce and a little lemon zest add zing to this chicken.

Here's what I learned about cooking breaded chicken in the waffle iron:

• It works! And with heat coming from both sides, it cooks quickly.

Here's what I learned about pounding chicken:

• Put the chicken in a zip-top bag (press the air out before sealing) first. Pounding the chicken in a bag prevents the problem of having raw chicken juice spattered about your kitchen.

• Don't use the back end of a knife to pound the chicken. (The sharp end still has to go somewhere, and it could easily be your hand.) While a kitchen mallet is built for the task, you can use a heavy frying pan, a cutting board, or a rolling pin.

If you want to get a bit of a rhythm going when you make this, put the first batch of chicken in the waffle iron and run the second batch through the coatings while the first batch cooks.

Make sure you get only the bright yellow zest of the lemon, rather than the bitter white pith below the skin. Of course, if it's spicy you're after, you can go nuts with the hot sauce.

INGREDIENTS

¾ cup all-purpose flour

2 large eggs

Hot sauce, such as Tabasco, to taste

1½ cups plain bread crumbs

¼ cup grated Parmesan cheese

Finely grated zest of 1 lemon

1 teaspoon salt

1 teaspoon freshly ground black pepper

2 cups marinara sauce (see Spaghetti and Waffled Meatballs, page 65, Steps 1 to 5)

4 boneless, skinless chicken cutlets (1½ pounds total)

Nonstick cooking spray

½ cup grated mozzarella cheese

Waffled Vegetables (recipe follows)

Fresh whole basil leaves (optional)

1 Preheat the waffle iron on medium.

2 Place the flour in a shallow bowl or deep plate. In a second shallow bowl or deep plate, beat the eggs with a few drops of hot sauce.

3 In a third shallow bowl or deep plate, combine the bread crumbs, Parmesan, and lemon zest. Add ½ teaspoon of the salt and ½ teaspoon of the pepper.

4 Bring the marinara sauce to a simmer in a small saucepan over medium-low heat.

5 Put a single layer of the chicken in a zip-top bag, set it on a flat surface, and press down on the chicken with a cutting board, rolling pin, or heavy frying pan, until the chicken is about ¼ inch thick.

6 Remove the chicken from the bag, place it on a clean cutting board, and sprinkle the remaining ½ teaspoon each of salt and pepper over it.

7 Repeat Steps 5 and 6 with the remaining chicken.

8 Dredge a chicken cutlet in the flour, shaking off any excess. Transfer it to the bowl with the egg and turn the chicken to coat. Allow the excess egg mixture to drip back into the bowl, then coat the chicken with the bread crumb mixture, pressing the mixture to the chicken so it sticks. Set it aside on a platter and repeat with the remaining chicken.

9 Coat both sides of the waffle iron grid with nonstick spray. Place the chicken in the waffle iron, close the lid, and cook until golden brown and cooked through, 4 minutes.

10 Top the chicken with the grated mozzarella and close the lid for 20 seconds to allow the cheese to melt. Remove the chicken from the waffle iron.

11 Ladle about ½ cup marinara sauce per portion onto a plate and then place the chicken on top of the sauce. Drizzle with a little more sauce, add the waffled vegetables to the plate, and garnish everything with the basil.

Waffled Vegetables

TIME: 10 minutes | **YIELD:** 4 servings

1 Preheat the waffle iron on medium.

2 Toss the zucchini and the pepper with the olive oil and salt in a large bowl.

3 Place as many vegetables as will fit on the waffle iron, close the lid, and cook until the zucchini has softened but is not mushy, 4 minutes.

4 Use silicone-tipped tongs to remove the vegetables, and place them on a serving plate.

5 Repeat Steps 3 and 4 with the remaining vegetables.

INGREDIENTS

2 medium zucchini (about 1 pound), cut into ½-inch-thick chunks

1 large red bell pepper (about ½ pound), stemmed, seeded, and cut into ¼-inch-wide strips

2 tablespoons extra-virgin olive oil

¼ teaspoon salt

Waffled Chicken Breast
Stuffed with Spinach, Pine Nuts, and Feta

IRON: Belgian or standard | **TIME:** 25 minutes | **YIELD:** Serves 4

Every bite has tender chicken wrapped around a cheesy, slightly nutty center.

This one might not be picture-perfect every time, but it will be delicious. If a little stuffing spills out of the chicken, or the chicken doesn't quite close after you stuff it, it's not a big deal. Press onward.

INGREDIENTS

2 ounces (about 1 cup) fresh baby spinach, finely chopped

2 ounces feta cheese, crumbled (about ½ cup)

2 tablespoons pine nuts, toasted (see headnote)

2 cloves garlic, minced

½ teaspoon dried thyme

Nonstick cooking spray

4 boneless, skinless chicken breast halves (about 6 ounces each)

½ teaspoon salt

½ teaspoon freshly ground black pepper

NOTE: Using baby spinach means you don't have to worry about picking through to remove large stems.

Part of making sure it's delicious is toasting the pine nuts to bring out their flavor. Place the pine nuts in a dry frying pan over medium-low heat to toast them. Shake frequently until the nuts are just fragrant and are barely turning brown, a couple of minutes. When they're done, remove them from the heat and pour them onto a plate to stop the cooking.

I Preheat the waffle iron on medium. Preheat the oven on its lowest setting.

2 Combine the spinach, cheese, nuts, garlic, and thyme in a small bowl. Smash them together with a fork until the filling is more cohesive and easier to handle. Coat both sides of the waffle iron grid with nonstick spray.

3 Make a horizontal cut into the thickest portion of each chicken breast half to form a pocket. Be careful not to cut all the way through. Divide the stuffing mixture into 4 portions and fill each pocket, leaving a margin at the edge so the pocket can close.

4 Season the chicken with salt and pepper. Place as many pieces as will fit in the waffle iron as far away from the hinge as possible. (This allows the lid to press down on the chicken more evenly.) Close the lid.

5 Cook the chicken for 7 minutes before checking it. If the breasts are thick, you may need to rotate the meat 180 degrees at this point and continue cooking for another 3 minutes. The chicken should be golden brown and no pink should remain inside. Cut into the thickest part to check, if necessary. (If you're using an instant-read thermometer, the internal temperature of the meat should reach 165°F.)

6 Remove the chicken from the waffle iron and repeat Step 5 with any remaining chicken. Keep cooked chicken warm in the oven.

7 Serve warm.

Fawaffle (Waffled Falafel) and Hummus

| **IRON:** Belgian or standard | **TIME:** 20 minutes, plus overnight soaking for chickpeas | **YIELD:** Serves 4 |

Not only is waffled falafel a healthier alternative to the deep-fried version, it's as delicious as it is fun to say.

NOTE: To time this recipe for simultaneous serving, waffle the falafel while you're finishing up the hummus.

I often have canned chickpeas on hand for making hummus or for tossing in salads, so I would love to use those canned chickpeas to make falafel. But there's a problem: They're too soft and too moist for this recipe. After a long soak, dried chickpeas yield a firmer and meatier ingredient more suited for falafel. When it comes to the hummus, though, softer chickpeas are fine, so it's easier to use canned.

Removing the skins from chickpeas is the key to creating incomparably smooth hummus. Is it tedious? A bit. Is it strictly necessary? Not strictly. It will take about 3 or 4 minutes to get 95 percent of the skins off, and another few minutes to go after the last 5 percent. I usually stop after the first 3 or 4 minutes. Whether skinned or not, the chickpeas must first be processed without any additional ingredients, until they're ground as finely as possible. Only then do you add everything else.

Adding flour to the falafel makes the result a bit lighter and more cakelike, but it's not much flour and you can leave it out if you'd like. The recipe still works beautifully.

INGREDIENTS

1 cup dried chickpeas, picked over and soaked in water overnight in the refrigerator

½ small onion, roughly chopped

3 cloves garlic

¼ cup chopped fresh flat-leaf parsley

2 tablespoons extra-virgin olive oil

2 tablespoons all-purpose flour

1 teaspoon salt

1 teaspoon ground cumin

½ teaspoon ground coriander

¼ teaspoon baking powder

¼ teaspoon freshly ground black pepper

¼ teaspoon cayenne pepper

Nonstick cooking spray

Perfectly Smooth Hummus (recipe follows)

4 pockets pita bread (optional)

NOTE: To time this recipe for simultaneous serving, waffle the falafel while you're finishing up the hummus.

If you're serving this with pita bread, heat that in the waffle iron, too. It will be ready in 15 seconds, and the result will be twice as waffled: warmed and waffled pita bread, filled with waffled falafel, topped with dollops of Perfectly Smooth Hummus, and served with tomatoes, cucumbers, and parsley with a drizzle of olive oil.

1 Preheat the waffle iron on medium. Preheat the oven on its lowest setting.

2 Drain the soaked chickpeas and place them with the onion and garlic in a food processor. Pulse until blended but not pureed.

3 Add the parsley, olive oil, flour, salt, cumin, coriander, baking powder, black pepper, and cayenne pepper, and pulse until mostly smooth.

4 Coat both sides of the waffle iron grid with nonstick spray. For each fawaffle, place about ¼ cup of batter in the waffle iron, leaving a bit of space between scoops for each to expand.

5 Close the lid of the waffle iron and cook for 5 minutes before checking. Remove the fawaffles when they are cooked through and evenly browned.

6 Repeat Steps 4 and 5 with the remaining batter.

7 Keep finished fawaffles warm in the oven. Serve them with the hummus and pita bread.

TIPS

• Falafel from a box? There's no shame in that. Prepare the falafel mix according to package directions. Be sure to let the mixture sit for 15 to 30 minutes to allow the dry ingredients to hydrate fully. Waffle as instructed above.

• Leftover falafel mixture can be stored in a covered bowl in the refrigerator for a few days. No need to let it come to room temperature—just add another minute or two to the cook time.

Perfectly Smooth Hummus

TIME: 20 minutes | **YIELD:** About 1½ cups; serves 4

1   Remove the skins from the chickpeas: Fill a large bowl with water, pour the chickpeas into the bowl, and rub them gently to pop off as many skins as you can. The skins float to the top, where they can be skimmed off. It's not necessary to get every last one off, so leave the stubborn ones.

2   In a food processor or with a blender, pulse the chickpeas until just pureed.

3   Add the garlic, ¼ teaspoon salt, olive oil, tahini, and lemon juice, and blend until smooth. Taste and add more salt or lemon juice, if desired. To adjust the consistency, add 1 tablespoon of olive oil or water at a time, pulsing to combine.

4   Serve with the fawaffles. Leftover hummus will keep in a covered container in the refrigerator for up to a week.

INGREDIENTS

1 can (15 ounces) chickpeas, drained and rinsed

1 small clove garlic, minced

Salt

¼ cup extra-virgin olive oil

¼ cup tahini

2 tablespoons fresh lemon juice, or more as needed

NOTE: You can substitute smooth, unsalted peanut butter for the tahini or eliminate it altogether. If you don't want to use tahini or peanut butter, reduce the lemon juice to 1 tablespoon.

Waffled Tuna Niçoise Salad

IRON: Belgian or standard | **TIME:** 45 minutes | **YIELD:** Serves 2

This makes an excellent light meal for a summer evening.

T his dish is utterly flexible. If you don't have an ingredient on hand, leave it out. No big deal.

This meal can also lay foundations for other meals. Boil extra eggs; they'll keep in the refrigerator for about a week in their shells. Boil extra potatoes; they'll keep in the refrigerator for a few days and can be turned into hash browns on the stove top.

Much of this recipe can be prepared the day before. Then, it's just a matter of cooking the tuna in the waffle iron and assembling the salad.

Oh, and let's talk about the elephant in the room—or rather, the fish in the waffle iron. Yes, you will be using your waffle iron to cook fish. The tuna stays intact and, in general, is not at all messy to cook in the waffle iron. Still, you'll want to clean it thoroughly before you cook breakfast in it.

INGREDIENTS

2 large eggs

½ cup green beans,
    with tips snipped

4 new potatoes, cut in half

Salt

Nonstick cooking spray

1 fresh tuna steak
    (about 8 ounces)

3 cups washed salad greens

¼ cup pitted or whole sliced
    black olives, such as
    Niçoise or kalamata

½ cup whole or halved
    cherry or grape tomatoes

Freshly ground black
    pepper, to taste

Dijon Vinaigrette Dressing,
    (recipe follows)

NOTE: The first three
steps can be done ahead,
anywhere from a few
hours before to 2 days.
Just refrigerate the eggs,
green beans, and potatoes
until you're ready to use
them.

1 Cook the eggs: Place the eggs in a small saucepan and fill it two-thirds full with water. Bring the water to a boil over medium-high heat, then turn off the heat, remove the saucepan from the burner, and cover it. Let it rest for 10 minutes. Run the eggs under cold water for a minute to cool them, and set aside.

2 Blanch the green beans: Bring a small saucepan of salted water to a boil, and plunge the green beans in for 30 seconds. Remove them and place them in an ice-water bath to stop the cooking. Remove the green beans from the ice water after 1 minute and set aside.

3 Boil the potatoes: Place the potatoes in a small saucepan and cover with at least an inch of water. Add a generous pinch of salt to the water and bring to a boil over medium-high heat. Once the water boils, reduce the heat to low and allow the potatoes to simmer for 10 minutes. They're ready when they can be pierced with the gentle poke of a knife. Remove the potatoes, drain them in a colander, and let cool.

4 Preheat the waffle iron on high. Coat both sides of the waffle iron grid with nonstick spray.

5 Place the tuna steak on the waffle iron as far away from the hinge as possible. (This allows the lid to press down on the tuna more evenly.) Close the lid.

6 While the tuna cooks, lay down a bed of salad greens on a large serving plate. Peel the eggs, slice or quarter them, and arrange them on the lettuce. Evenly distribute the green beans, potatoes, olives, and tomatoes on the salad greens.

7 Check on the tuna. After 6 minutes, a ¾-inch-thick steak should be cooked through. There should be no pink on the exterior. You may wish to cut the tuna in half to see if any pink remains in the center. A pink tinge can be okay, though you may prefer your tuna more well done. (The USDA recommends that it reach 145°F on an instant-read thermometer; I like mine around 125°F.)

8 Remove the tuna from the waffle iron and cut it into slices about ½ inch thick. Arrange the slices on the salad, with the waffle marks facing up.

9 Sprinkle the salad with salt and pepper. Dress the salad sparingly. Serve the rest of the dressing at the table.

Dijon Vinaigrette Dressing

In a small bowl, whisk together the olive oil, vinegar, and mustard until well combined.

(Or shake the ingredients in a jar with a lid.) Taste and add salt and pepper as necessary.

INGREDIENTS

½ cup extra-virgin olive oil

2 teaspoons distilled white vinegar

½ teaspoon Dijon mustard

Salt and freshly ground black pepper, to taste

Waffled Salmon
with Miso-Maple Glaze and Asparagus

IRON: Belgian or standard | **TIME:** 15 minutes | **YIELD:** Serves 2

Try wild salmon for a meatier texture and more assertive flavor.

The salty, fermented tang of miso and the sweetness of maple syrup lend this dish a complex flavor without too much fuss.

I tried adding the glaze when the salmon first goes in the waffle iron but the sugars in the maple syrup burned, the garlic toasted too much, and the whole thing started throwing off smoke. However, I needed a little heat to marry the glaze to the fish. The solution? Cook the salmon until just before it's done, then brush on the glaze for the last minute or so of waffling.

To store fresh ginger, keep it in a zip-top bag in your refrigerator's vegetable crisper. It should keep about a month.

1 In a small bowl, whisk together the maple syrup, miso, vinegar, sesame oil, ginger, and garlic. Set the mixture aside.

2 Preheat the waffle iron on high. Coat both sides of the waffle iron grid with nonstick spray.

3 Place the salmon (skin-side down, if it has skin) on the waffle iron and close the lid. While the fish is cooking, toss the asparagus with the olive oil and season with salt and pepper in another bowl.

4 After 4 minutes, check on the fish. The salmon should be close to done. You should see no translucence on the edges. If your fillets are thicker than ½ inch or you're unsure about whether the salmon is done, use a small, sharp knife to cut a small incision in the middle of the salmon. You should see only a trace of translucence in the middle. (The USDA recommends it reach an internal temperature of 145°F as measured on an instant-read thermometer; I like mine about 135°F.)

5 Use a silicone brush to baste the salmon with the glaze, close the lid, and cook until the glaze becomes sticky, 1 minute more.

6 Remove the fish from the waffle iron, place the asparagus spears in the waffle iron, and close the lid.

7 Cook the asparagus until just tender, 3 minutes. Thinner spears will finish cooking first. Remove the spears as they finish.

8 Serve the asparagus alongside the salmon. If you have extra glaze, strain the garlic from it and serve it on the side or drizzle it over the fish.

INGREDIENTS

1 tablespoon maple syrup

2 teaspoons yellow miso paste

1 teaspoon distilled white vinegar

1 teaspoon pure sesame oil

½ teaspoon grated fresh ginger

1 clove garlic, minced

Nonstick cooking spray

2 salmon fillets (4 to 6 ounces each), ½ inch thick, with or without skin

8 ounces asparagus (about 12 spears), washed and with tough bottom ends removed

¼ cup extra-virgin olive oil

Salt and freshly ground black pepper, to taste

TIP

Use any extra miso as a soup base; in a salad dressing with a neutral oil such as canola, a bit of honey, and a few drops of sesame oil; or with mayonnaise for use as a dipping sauce. Add a bit at a time and taste as you go.

VARIATIONS

• Spice up the glaze by adding a few drops of chili paste or hot sauce to it.

• Substitute an equal amount of soy sauce for the miso paste.

Waffled Calamari Salad
with Thai Dressing

IRON: Standard (Belgian may be used, but take care to arrange the squid on the iron for maximum number of waffle marks)	**TIME:** 10 minutes	**YIELD:** Serves 2

When I'm trying to illustrate the idea that the waffle iron is so much more than waffles, squid usually do the trick.

Squid don't take long to cook, and the high heat of the waffle iron is perfect for the task. Squid are ranked as a "good alternative" in the Monterey Bay Aquarium's sustainable seafood listings. They're also relatively inexpensive, especially when sold frozen. (The squid that are not sold frozen are usually previously frozen, so if you're able to plan ahead, you can save money by buying from the freezer case.) Squid are usually sold cleaned, with the beak and ink sac removed.

Thai cuisine knows how to strike a balance among sweet, sour, spicy, and salty notes. This recipe—with its lime juice, sugar, fish sauce, and hot peppers—is an excellent example.

INGREDIENTS

Nonstick cooking spray

8 ounces cleaned squid, bodies and tentacles

½ small red onion, thinly sliced

2 tablespoons roasted peanuts, crushed

Thai Dressing (recipe follows)

1 sprig cilantro, large stems removed, for garnish

Thai bird chile peppers or other small chile peppers, for garnish (optional)

NOTE: Thai bird chile peppers brighten the plate but can be quite fiery. Using them is optional and eating them is *extra* optional.

1 Preheat the waffle iron on high.

2 Coat both sides of the waffle iron grid with nonstick spray. Arrange the squid on the waffle iron without crowding, close the lid, and cook until the squid are opaque, about 2 minutes.

3 When the squid have finished cooking, allow them to cool slightly on a cutting board, then cut the bodies into strips about 1 inch wide. The tentacles can remain whole.

4 To serve, arrange the squid on a plate with the onion slices, top with the crushed peanuts, and drizzle with the Thai Dressing. Garnish with the cilantro and chiles.

INGREDIENTS

2 tablespoons lime juice

2 tablespoons fish sauce

1 teaspoon red pepper flakes

1 teaspoon sugar

Pinch of salt

Thai Dressing

Combine the lime juice, fish sauce, red pepper flakes, sugar, and salt in a small bowl and set aside.

Leftover fish sauce? Add just a dash to tomato or marinara sauce to give it more depth of flavor and a faint, pleasant, briny note.

Crisscrossed Crab Cakes

IRON: Belgian or standard | **TIME:** 20 minutes | **YIELD:** Makes 4 crab cakes

The richness of the generous lumps of crabmeat cuts the spice of the sauce.

What's your ideal crab cake? Does it taste like bread crumbs or crackers? I'm not even waiting for your answer. It tastes like crab.

But this is where we run up against science: Your crab cake needs something to hold it together. This is where the egg comes in. (Of course, you could just put a whole crab in the waffle iron—see Waffled Soft-Shell Crab, page 108.)

Eggs are often called "binders" in a recipe because they hold together the components, preventing the whole ensemble from falling apart under the heat. Bread crumbs help soak up some of the moisture and prevent the recipe from becoming a waffled crab omelet (not that there is a single thing wrong with that).

The trick is to use as little egg and as few bread crumbs as you can get away with. And that's what testing this recipe meant—finding the bare minimum necessary to avoid an unholy mess. (You're welcome.) Once your crab cakes are safely out of the waffle iron, use lemon slices and Sriracha Mayonnaise to brighten the flavor. To make them a meal, serve with lightly dressed greens or on a roll as a sandwich.

Oh, also, I guess it bears mentioning: You're cooking seafood in a waffle iron. Without proper cleaning, the next thing you cook in that waffle iron might also taste like seafood. Maybe you should buy a waffle iron dedicated to seafood? Or, you know, just clean your waffle iron.

1 Preheat the waffle iron on high. Preheat the oven on its lowest setting.

2 In a small bowl, mix the egg, cayenne pepper, and black pepper. Set aside.

3 In a medium-size bowl, gently combine the crab, bread crumbs, bell pepper, and chopped shallot. Add the egg mixture, stirring gently to incorporate it evenly into the dry ingredients.

4 Coat both sides of the waffle iron grid with nonstick spray. With a measuring cup, scoop out ½ cup of the mixture and place it in the waffle iron. Close the lid and cook until the bread crumbs are golden brown and no liquid remains, about 3 minutes.

5 Remove the crab cake from the waffle iron, spritz it with a lemon slice, and use the extra slices as garnish.

6 Repeat Steps 4 and 5 to make the remaining 3 crab cakes. Keep the finished crab cakes warm in the oven.

7 Dollop a tablespoon of the Sriracha Mayonnaise on each crab cake, and serve.

INGREDIENTS

1 large egg, beaten, with a pinch of salt

Pinch of cayenne pepper or curry powder

½ teaspoon freshly ground black pepper or lemon pepper

1½ cups lump crab (about 10 ounces)

½ cup plain bread crumbs

¼ cup finely chopped green bell pepper

1 tablespoon chopped shallot

Nonstick cooking spray

1 lemon, sliced, for garnish

¼ cup Sriracha Mayonnaise, for serving (recipe follows)

Sriracha Mayonnaise

Combine 2 drops of Sriracha with the mayonnaise in a small bowl. Taste for spiciness and add more Sriracha, if desired.

INGREDIENTS

Chili sauce, such as Sriracha, to taste

¼ cup mayonnaise

Waffled Soft-Shell Crab

IRON: Belgian or standard | **TIME:** 15 minutes | **YIELD:** Serves 2

For a complete meal, serve with coleslaw, or on a bun with mayonnaise and slices of ripe tomato.

Soft-shell crab season runs from midspring through early fall, when blue crabs molt and their new outer shells haven't yet hardened. In season, you can often buy live soft-shells at fish counters—look for crabs that are still kicking a bit if you prod them. The rest of the year, they're available frozen.

Frozen crabs are usually sold precleaned, but the fresh ones first need to be "dressed," or cleaned, and the fishmonger will often offer to do so. Word to the wise: Take him up on it.

I had a hard time finding crabs, because I had just moved to Montreal and didn't quite know my way around. Time was running out to test this recipe.

Alberto saved me.

On Monday morning I was on the phone with him, a very nice gentleman fishmonger in Southern California, which, despite being on the opposite coast from crab country, was the location of the only business I could find willing to ship crabs to Canada.

On Wednesday morning I answered the door in my pajamas. It was the UPS man with a box full of crabs.

In between, the crabs spent a night in a customs holding warehouse. Panicked at the thought of melting crabs, I called to see

INGREDIENTS

½ cup all-purpose flour

1 teaspoon seafood
seasoning mix,
such as Old Bay

2 soft-shell crabs,
cleaned ("dressed")

2 tablespoons unsalted
butter, melted

NOTE: If the crabs have
not been cleaned: Lay
down some newspaper to
make for easier cleanup.
Place a crab right side up
on the newspaper and use
kitchen shears to cut away
the face, about ½ inch
behind the eyes. Then, lift
up the left and right sides
of the top shell and scrape
out or cut the fringed
white or gray gills.Turn
the crab over and remove
the apron. Repeat with the
remaining crab.

whether the crabs could be placed in the refrigerator or freezer. ("No.")
But it's okay. The crabs arrived in excellent shape.

Alberto is the man.

This recipe is simple and unadorned. Part of the pleasure of a soft-shell crab is letting nothing come between you and the crab, except maybe a squeeze of fresh lemon.

1 Preheat the waffle iron on high.

2 In a shallow bowl or deep dish, such as a pie plate, combine the flour and seasoning mix.

3 Pat a crab dry with paper towels. Dredge the crab in the flour, shake off the excess flour over the plate, and set aside the coated crab on a cutting board.

4 Using a silicone brush, coat both sides of the waffle iron grid with the melted butter.

5 Place the coated crab on the waffle iron, close the lid, and cook for 3 minutes. The coating should turn golden brown. If any raw flour remains on the crab, brush that spot with butter and continue to cook for another 30 seconds or so.

6 Repeat Steps 3 through 5 with the remaining crab.

Bibimbaffle
(Waffled Bibimbap)

IRON: Belgian or standard | **TIME:** 20 minutes | **YIELD:** Serves 2

Traditionally, bibimbap is a mix of vegetables and meat sitting on a bed of steamed rice—the rice is not waffled.

Matt Troost is the man behind bibimbaffle, and when I first met him he was working at a restaurant with an Italian menu. You might have expected waffled pizza. He gave us waffled Korean food.

In this version, kimchee and an egg are laid atop rice that's been waffled with vegetable banchan (seasoned vegetables). The faint, nutty sweetness of the rice hits the tang of the kimchee. The heat of the hot pepper paste meets the comforting familiarity of the egg yolk.

Are some of these ingredients going to require a trip to an Asian market? Maybe. But you can do what Matt does: Keep the vegetables, sesame oil, soy sauce, kimchee, and hot pepper paste on hand for simple, quick meals. From there, it's just a matter of having two staples: rice and eggs.

Despite your best intentions, the rice may not come out in one piece—that's not a problem. Pick out the best piece and leave it uncovered. Hide the other pieces under the kimchee, vegetables, or egg.

No one needs to know.

1   Preheat the waffle iron on medium and use a silicone brush to coat both sides of the grid with sesame oil.

2   Place ½ cup rice on the waffle iron and distribute it evenly. Sprinkle about half of the vegetables on the rice, and then cover with another ½ cup rice, evenly distributed.

3   Close the lid of the waffle iron and cook until the rice is crispy, about 8 minutes. Repeat Step 2 with the remaining rice and veggies, using another coat of sesame oil if needed.

4   While the rice and vegetables are cooking, fry the egg (or, for a fully waffled meal, wait until the rice is done to waffle an egg, following the instructions in Crispy Waffled Bacon and Eggs, page 14): Place a nonstick pan over high heat and fry an egg sunny side up until it's crispy on the bottom and soft on top, about 1 minute. Remove the egg from the pan and season it with salt and pepper. Repeat with the second egg.

5   Assemble your plate with the crispy waffled rice on bottom, the egg on top, a spoonful or more of hot pepper paste as a garnish, and a generous spoonful of kimchee on the side. Season with a splash or two of soy sauce and serve.

INGREDIENTS

1 tablespoon pure sesame oil

2 cups cooked white rice

½ cup vegetable banchan, drained

2 large eggs

Salt and freshly ground black pepper, to taste

Gochujang (hot pepper paste), to taste

½ cup kimchee

Soy sauce, for drizzling (optional)

NOTE: Banchan (side dishes) are available prepackaged at most Korean markets and some grocery stores.

TIP

Leftover ingredients? Use the vegetables, kimchee, or hot pepper paste in your next stir-fry.

Waffled Tamale Pie

IRON: Belgian or standard (Belgian will yield a better topping-to-crust ratio)	**TIME:** 30 minutes	**YIELD:** Serves 4

This recipe takes a cornmeal crust and builds on it. What you build is up to you.

My favorite version of Waffled Tamale Pie is a Southwestern-style beef filling topped with sharp Cheddar cheese. But your topping can be tweaked according to what you have on hand. Leftover taco filling? Sure. Shredded chicken from the night before? No problem. Pinto beans and tomatoes? Go for it.

I went into this recipe knowing I wanted it to be more than merely a topping plopped on a cornmeal crust. I wanted the two to become one. Here's how I wanted it to work: You put the crust dough in the waffle iron, but don't close the lid. Magically, the bottom cooks completely and the top partially cooks. When you top it with the beef and tomato mixture, you close the lid and everything melds beautifully.

In my dreams.

The problem is that leaving the top open like that meant the top of the cornmeal crust received no heat at all. Even the bottom barely cooked. Without the lid to press down on the mixture, it just sat atop the grid. After 3 minutes of cooking, the crust was still raw.

So, it was back to the drawing board.

Here's what worked: Cook the crust with the lid closed until it is just golden brown and then warm up the topping with another go-round. For a grace note, the cheese is melted with just a quick bit of heat.

INGREDIENTS

Topping:

1 tablespoon extra-virgin
   olive oil

1 large onion, finely chopped

1 pound ground turkey
   or beef

1 jalapeño pepper, minced
   (remove seeds for less
   heat)

1 teaspoon ground cumin

1 can (15 ounces) crushed
   tomatoes

Salt and freshly ground
   black pepper, to taste

Crust:

1½ cups masa harina

1 teaspoon salt

1 teaspoon baking powder

¼ teaspoon freshly ground
   black pepper

1 cup milk

4 tablespoons (½ stick)
   unsalted butter, melted

1 large egg, beaten

Nonstick cooking spray

1 cup shredded sharp
   Cheddar cheese

NOTE: Masa harina can be
found in a supermarket's
baking or Mexican foods
aisle.

The crust should be made just before you're ready to cook it. It comes together quickly. The topping can be prepared ahead of time and refrigerated for a day or two—it will give you leftovers. Serve it in tacos, on nachos, or simply on its own alongside a salad.

1 Make the topping: Place the olive oil in a large frying pan and add the onion. Sauté over medium heat until the onion just begins to brown, about 5 minutes. Remove the onion and set it aside on a plate.

2 Crumble the meat into the same skillet, browning it until no traces of pink remain, about 5 minutes. Pour off the excess fat and add the sautéed onion, jalapeño, cumin, and tomatoes to the pan until just heated through, about 1 minute. Taste and add salt and pepper. Let the mixture simmer over low heat while making the crust.

3 Preheat the waffle iron on medium.

4 Make the crust: In a large bowl, combine the masa harina, salt, baking powder, and black pepper. In a medium-size bowl, whisk the milk and the melted butter until combined, then whisk in the egg.

5 Add the wet ingredients to the dry ingredients and stir to combine. The batter will be very thick.

6 Coat both sides of the waffle iron grid with nonstick spray. Divide the dough into 4 equal portions, about ½ cup each. Take a portion of the dough and pat it into a disk about the size of one section of the waffle iron. Repeat with the remaining 3 portions of dough.

7 Place the disks on the waffle iron, covering the waffle iron grid completely. Close the lid and cook until mostly set but not quite golden brown, about 3 minutes.

8 Open the waffle iron, spoon an even layer of the topping roughly ½ inch thick across the crust, and close the waffle iron for 1 minute. Open the waffle iron once more, top with the cheese, and close the waffle iron for 20 seconds to melt the cheese. Remove the tamale pies from the waffle iron and serve.

VARIATIONS

- Add ½ cup shredded sharp Cheddar cheese to the crust.
- Only so much waffling in you? Cook the crust in the waffle iron and serve the topping in a bowl, chili style, with the masa waffle on the side.

TIPS

- To freeze the leftover topping: Once the topping has cooled, place it in a large zip-top bag, and spread the topping in a thin, even layer, pressing flat to remove any air. Store it in the freezer. When you're ready to use the topping, break off a piece, and place it on top of the cooked crust in Step 8.

- To freeze the leftover crust: You can cook the crust and then freeze the resulting waffles in a zip-top bag, or you can wrap the uncooked dough in plastic wrap and store the wrapped dough in a zip-top bag in the freezer. Allow the dough to thaw in the refrigerator before waffling.

Waffled Mexican Migas

IRON: Belgian or standard | **TIME:** 15 minutes | **YIELD:** Serves 2

This recipe is as good for dealing with leftovers as it is hangovers. I've heard.

INGREDIENTS

4 large eggs

1 small tomato, diced (about ½ cup)

½ cup diced onion

½ cup shredded Cheddar or Monterey Jack cheese

1 small jalapeño pepper, seeded and minced

2 soft corn tortillas, cut or torn into about ½-inch pieces

¼ teaspoon salt

¼ teaspoon freshly ground black pepper

Nonstick cooking spray

Working with jalapeños can be tricky, but it's easy to emerge unscathed. There are a million tips on how to get the sting out of your hands—dousing your hands with ketchup, soaking them in yogurt, spritzing them with lemon juice. Just about everything but jalapeño juice has been recommended. I don't know if any of those methods work.

What does work is a little prevention. Wear gloves when you're cutting the jalapeño. If you don't have gloves, be very careful about what you touch after you cut it. If you're like me, you won't remember you've been cutting a jalapeño until you touch your finger to your face and remember two things:

1. You've been cutting a jalapeño, and . . .

2. . . . You told yourself not to touch your eyes and now you've gone and done it, genius.

1 Preheat the waffle iron on medium.

2 In a medium-size bowl, beat the eggs. Add the rest of the ingredients except the cooking spray and stir vigorously to combine.

3 Coat both sides of the waffle iron grid with nonstick spray. Ladle some of the mixture onto each section of the waffle iron. Some ingredients may settle to the bottom of the bowl, so make sure you reach to the bottom of the bowl to get a good mixture.

4 Close the lid and cook until the eggs are no longer runny, 2 minutes.

5 Remove the migas from the waffle iron with an offset spatula or a pair of heat-resistant silicon spatulas, and serve.

VARIATIONS

• For a substantial meal, serve with refried beans, along with soft corn or flour tortillas heated for 10 seconds in the waffle iron.

• Swap out the tomato or onion for pretty much any diced vegetable. Or keep both onion and tomato and add up to ½ cup of another vegetable.

• To dress it up, garnish with salsa, cheese, sour cream, sliced avocado, or scallions.

Chapter 4

Snacks, Sides, and Small Bites

Waffled Chicken Fingers

IRON: Belgian or standard | **TIME:** 30 minutes | **YIELD:** Serves 4

And you thought ordinary chicken fingers were popular with kids . . .

Finding one recipe that can do double duty as Chicken Parmesan (page 86) and—with just a few more ingredients—turn into Chicken Fingers was a big win.

When it comes to the dipping sauces, using a base of mayonnaise means it's not too difficult to whip up two different options.

1 Preheat the waffle iron on medium.

2 Place the flour in a shallow bowl or deep plate. In a second shallow bowl or deep plate, beat the eggs with a few drops of hot sauce.

3 In a third shallow bowl or deep plate, combine the bread crumbs, Parmesan, and lemon zest. Add ½ teaspoon of the salt and ½ teaspoon of the pepper and stir to combine.

4 Put a single layer of the chicken in a zip-top bag, set it on a flat surface, and press down on the chicken with a cutting board, rolling pin, or heavy frying pan. Pound the chicken to a thickness of about ¼ inch. Remove the chicken from the bag and cut it into strips about an inch wide. Repeat with the remaining chicken.

5 Season the chicken strips with the remaining ½ teaspoon each of the salt and pepper.

INGREDIENTS

¾ cup all-purpose flour

2 large eggs

Hot sauce, such as Tabasco, to taste

1½ cups plain bread crumbs

¼ cup grated Parmesan cheese

Finely grated zest of 1 lemon

1 teaspoon salt

1 teaspoon freshly ground black pepper

1½ pounds boneless, skinless chicken cutlets

Nonstick cooking spray

Dipping sauces (recipes follow)

Working in batches, dredge it in the flour, shaking off any excess. Transfer it to the bowl with the egg and turn the chicken to coat.

6 Allow the excess egg mixture to drip back into the bowl, then coat the chicken with the bread crumb mixture, pressing the mixture so it sticks.

7 Coat both sides of the waffle iron grid with nonstick spray. Place the chicken in the waffle iron, close the lid, and cook until golden brown and cooked through, 4 minutes.

8 Remove the chicken from the waffle iron and serve with sauces of your choice.

INGREDIENTS

¼ cup mayonnaise

2 tablespoons honey

1 tablespoon Dijon mustard

Honey Mustard Dipping Sauce

Combine the mayonnaise, honey, and Dijon mustard in a small bowl and stir thoroughly.

INGREDIENTS

¼ cup mayonnaise

¼ teaspoon hot sauce, such as Tabasco (or to taste)

Spicy Mayonnaise Dipping Sauce

Combine the mayonnaise and the hot sauce in a small bowl and stir thoroughly. Taste and add more hot sauce, if desired.

Sweet-and-Sour Waffled Shrimp Wontons

IRON: Belgian or standard | **TIME:** 45 minutes | **YIELD:** Makes 16 wontons

The waffle iron is many things, but it is not a steamer.

Maybe you're getting clever and thinking: I could add a little bit of water to the waffle iron and steam these dumplings! You could. But you shouldn't.

See, I have already tried out the steaming theory for you. First, I added 1 tablespoon of water to the waffle iron and stood back as the steam whooshed upward. Then I added the wontons. The results were about the same as without adding the water. To have a meaningful effect, you would have to add water throughout the cooking process; it's not really practical and it's not worth it.

These wontons will have a slight tang without being overwhelmingly sour. Serve them with the Ginger-Sesame Dipping Sauce (page 128), or with soy sauce, a sweet-and-sour sauce, or a little toasted sesame oil.

TIP

Assembled wontons may be frozen and waffled later. To freeze, place the wontons in a single layer on a tray or baking sheet covered with parchment paper. Place the tray in the freezer for 30 minutes, then remove it, put the wontons in a zip-top bag, and return the bag to the freezer. To reheat, remove wontons from the freezer 45 minutes before cooking and allow them to return to room temperature under a damp cloth or paper towel.

1 Finely chop the shrimp so that they end up as almost a paste. If you want to use a food processor, a half dozen quick pulses should accomplish this. Place the chopped shrimp in a medium-size bowl.

2 Add the egg white, scallion, garlic, sugar, vinegar, ginger, salt, and pepper to the shrimp, stir to mix thoroughly, and set aside.

3 Preheat the waffle iron on high. Preheat the oven on its lowest setting.

4 To form the dumplings, remove a wonton wrapper from the package. Using a pastry brush or a clean finger, wet all 4 edges of the wrapper. Place a scant tablespoon of the shrimp mixture in the center and top with another wonton wrapper. Press along the edges to seal. The water should act as glue. If you find a spot that's not sticking, add a bit more water. Set aside the finished wonton, cover with a damp towel, and shape the rest.

5 Coat both sides of the waffle iron grid with nonstick spray. Set as many wontons on the waffle iron as will comfortably fit and close the lid. Cook for 2 minutes before checking. The wonton wrapper should lose its translucency and the waffle marks should be deep golden brown. This may take up to 4 minutes. Remove the cooked wontons and keep them warm in the oven while the others cook.

6 Serve the wontons with the Ginger-Sesame Dipping Sauce.

INGREDIENTS

8 ounces cooked and chilled shrimp (31–40 count or 41–50 count), peeled, tails removed

1 large egg white, lightly beaten

¼ cup finely chopped scallion, both green and white parts

1 clove garlic, minced

2 teaspoons light brown sugar

2 teaspoons distilled white vinegar

½ teaspoon grated or minced fresh ginger

¾ teaspoon salt

½ teaspoon freshly ground black pepper

1 package wonton wrappers (at least 32 wrappers), about 3½ inches per side

Nonstick cooking spray

Ginger-Sesame Dipping Sauce (recipe follows)

NOTE: Shrimp are sold by size, with "31–40" count meaning that 31 to 40 shrimp fit in a pound.

INGREDIENTS

3 tablespoons soy sauce

2 teaspoons rice vinegar

½ teaspoon sesame oil

½ teaspoon grated fresh ginger

¼ teaspoon garlic-chili paste or Sriracha

Pinch of freshly ground black pepper

Ginger-Sesame Dipping Sauce

In a small bowl, whisk together the soy sauce, rice vinegar, sesame oil, and ginger. Add the garlic-chili paste, then whisk again and taste. If you want a bit more heat, add more chili paste. Extra sauce can be kept in a covered container in the refrigerator for a week.

Crispy Sesame Waffled Kale

IRON: Belgian or standard | **TIME:** 30 minutes | **YIELD:** Serves 2

I wasn't sure this one would work, and that's saying something, considering the things I've tossed into a waffle iron.

Cast your mind back to the early twenty-first century.... Had you heard of kale? Possibly you had. Was it flying off supermarket shelves? No.

INGREDIENTS

1 bunch kale, washed
and thoroughly dried,
thick stems removed

2 teaspoons sesame oil
blend or neutral-flavored
oil, such as canola or
grapeseed, mixed with a
few drops pure sesame oil

Kosher salt, to taste

NOTE: Curly or flat-leafed kale will work.

Kale is the little cruciferous vegetable that could. It has caught on in a way that cabbage never did. (No one is pushing cabbage as a superfood. Yet.) I like kale, but working new vegetables into your routine can be a little daunting. That's where kale chips come in. The leaves of kale come out satisfyingly crispy and slightly dimpled by the grid of the waffle iron.

Kale can trap dirt in its wrinkled leaves, so it's important to wash it well. It's also important to dry the kale thoroughly, or it will steam in the waffle iron and won't get crispy. A salad spinner works well for this task. Some supermarkets carry bagged kale already washed and prepared. The kale will cook down significantly, so start with more than you might think you need.

Sesame oil is available toasted and untoasted. Either one works in this recipe. Pure sesame oil is potent, so it's sometimes sold diluted. If your sesame oil is undiluted, you'll want to dilute it with a neutral-flavored oil.

1 Preheat the waffle iron on medium.

2 In a large bowl, toss the kale with the oil to coat.

3 Place as much of the kale as will fit in the waffle iron, covering the grid. Some overlap is fine, so don't worry too much about placing it in a single layer. The kale will cook down considerably, so it need not all lie flat; the pressure of the waffle iron lid will see to that.

4 Close the waffle iron lid for 30 seconds, then open and redistribute the kale for a more even layer. Close the lid again. After 8 minutes, check on the kale. Some pieces may finish before others. Remove those pieces and place them on a plate. It may take up to 15 minutes for the kale to become crispy and chiplike.

5 Repeat Steps 3 and 4 with the remaining kale.

6 Sprinkle with salt and serve.

Use a neutral-flavored oil, such as canola or grapeseed, in Step 2 and sprinkle the finished kale with any of the following:

• Seasoning salt • Cumin • Smoked paprika • Lemon pepper • Chili powder with a squeeze of lime • Sesame seeds

Caprese Salad with Waffled Eggplant

IRON: Belgian or standard	**TIME:** 40 minutes, including 30 minutes for salting eggplant	**YIELD:** Serves 2

Eggplant and tomatoes are two of summer's greatest gifts.

I attempted this recipe with both salted and unsalted eggplant. Salting removes some of the moisture and bitterness from the eggplant, but the biggest difference was what should have been obvious: The salted eggplant was better seasoned than the unsalted, even once the salt had been washed off. Salting is worth it if you have the time. If you're short on time, skip that step and try to use a smaller eggplant, because it's less likely to be bitter. Also, you may wish to let the cheese stand on the counter to come to room temperature while you salt the eggplant.

INGREDIENTS

1 small eggplant, cut into round slices about ½ inch thick

Kosher salt or coarse sea salt and freshly ground black pepper, to taste

2 medium-size ripe tomatoes

4 ounces fresh mozzarella

¼ cup extra-virgin olive oil, plus more for drizzling

1 large bunch basil, washed and dried, stems removed

1 Place the eggplant slices on a layer of paper towels and generously sprinkle both sides of the slices with salt. Allow the eggplant to sit for 30 minutes.

2 Meanwhile, slice the tomatoes into rounds. Do the same with the mozzarella.

3 Preheat the waffle iron on high.

4 Rinse the eggplant slices in cold water to wash off the salt. Pat the slices dry. Brush both sides of each eggplant slice with olive oil.

5 Place the eggplant in the waffle iron, close the lid, and cook until the eggplant is soft and cooked through, 4 minutes.

6 Remove the eggplant from the waffle iron and set on a serving plate, layering it with slices of tomatoes and cheese. Scatter the basil leaves atop the salad. Drizzle with olive oil and sprinkle with salt and freshly ground pepper.

VARIATIONS

• Serve with sliced red onions, olives, and capers

• For a spectacularly colorful presentation, choose heirloom tomatoes with varying tones.

Waffletons (Waffled Croutons)

IRON: Belgian or standard (the larger grid of a Belgian-style iron produces croutons with a more satisfying heft)	**TIME:** 30 minutes	**YIELD:** 8 cups; serves 8

When you begin incorporating waffles into salads, you know you're a true believer.

There are two paths to waffled croutons: Take leftover waffles and transform them into croutons in the oven, or take cubes of bread (shown) and transform them into croutons in the waffle iron.

I'm happy to report that either way produces great results.

Most waffles have a subtle sweetness. Offsetting this with the sharpness of Parmesan, garlic, and pepper tweaks them back into savory territory. This savory combination works well for plain bread, too. The type of bread is flexible. A brioche creates rich, slightly sweet croutons. Sandwich bread is more of a blank slate. A baguette will work, too, but be sure to trim the crusts first.

INGREDIENTS

3 slices thick bread, or 2 Belgian-style waffles, cut into cubes

2 cloves garlic

½ cup extra-virgin olive oil

1 tablespoon grated Parmesan cheese

Pinch of salt

¼ teaspoon freshly ground black pepper

1 If you're using bread, preheat the waffle iron on medium. If you're using waffles, preheat the oven to 450°F.

2 Crush the garlic cloves with the flat side of a knife blade. Place the garlic and the cubed bread or waffles in a medium-size bowl with the oil, cheese,

salt, and pepper. Stir to combine. Allow everything to soak for 5 minutes, toss, and then allow to soak another 5 minutes.

3 **IF YOU'RE USING BREAD:** Place the soaked bread cubes in the preheated waffle iron, close the lid, and cook for 5 minutes before checking on them. The waffled croutons are done when they are mostly golden brown, though the waffle indentations may be darker brown.

IF YOU'RE USING WAFFLES: Arrange the soaked waffle cubes on a baking sheet or in a cast-iron skillet and place in the preheated oven. Cook for 10 minutes, turning the cubes over with a spatula about halfway through and keeping an eye on them during the final 3 minutes to avoid burning. They should be a deep golden brown when finished, perhaps with a few blackened tips.

4 Serve the croutons with your favorite salad or sprinkle them on top of tomato soup.

VARIATIONS

- Add ¼ teaspoon dried oregano and ¼ teaspoon dried basil to the olive oil mixture in Step 2.

- Substitute an equal amount of Asiago or Pecorino Romano for the Parmesan.
- Add ¼ teaspoon red pepper flakes to the olive oil.

Waffled Pajeon
(Korean Scallion Pancake)

IRON: Belgian or standard | **TIME:** 10 minutes | **YIELD:** Serves 4

Make this recipe once. If you like it, grow one of the ingredients yourself for the next time.

This recipe calls for just the green parts of the scallions. But here's the secret that Big Scallion doesn't want you to know: The scallions will grow—and grow like mad—if you put about 2 inches of the white parts, root side down, in a jar with about 1 inch of water and leave the jar on a windowsill or on a counter where it can get some sun. It will be a while before you need to buy scallions again.

The dipping sauce calls for toasted sesame seeds. You can often find sesame seeds sold already toasted. Toasting them yourself is easy but involves walking a thin line—perfectly toasted turns to tragically burnt in a flash.

To toast the seeds, place a small frying pan over medium heat and add the sesame seeds to the dry, heated pan. Shake the pan occasionally to move the sesame seeds around. Cook for about 2 minutes. When the seeds are fragrant and just beginning to turn brown, remove them from the pan, spread on a plate, and allow to cool.

INGREDIENTS

1 cup all-purpose flour

1½ teaspoons granulated sugar

1 teaspoon salt

1 cup water

10 scallions, washed and dried

Nonstick cooking spray

Sesame-Soy Dipping Sauce (recipe follows)

1 | Preheat the waffle iron on medium.

2 | In a medium-size bowl, combine the flour, sugar, and salt. Add the water and whisk just until combined.

3 Trim away the white bottoms of the scallions. (See the headnote for what to do with the white parts.) Trim the tops of the scallions if they are ragged and sad. Cut the stems so that they are roughly the length of one section of your waffle iron.

4 Coat both sides of the waffle iron grid with nonstick spray. Arrange a small handful of scallions on the waffle iron. For the best-looking pajeon, set the scallions in the "valleys" of the waffle iron and arrange them in a crisscross pattern. Pour about ¼ cup of batter on top and close the waffle iron.

5 Cook until the batter has set and the scallions have cooked through, 4 minutes. You can poke one of the scallions with the tip of a sharp knife to see if it has cooked.

6 Remove the pajeon from the waffle iron and repeat Steps 4 and 5 with the remaining scallions and batter.

7 Serve with the Sesame-Soy Dipping Sauce.

VARIATION

Waffled Pajeon can be made with other vegetables. Cut zucchini or carrots into strips about the thickness of a matchstick and use in place of the scallions.

Sesame-Soy Dipping Sauce

Place the soy sauce, rice wine vinegar, honey, and sesame seeds in a small bowl, stir to combine, and set the sauce aside.

INGREDIENTS

2 tablespoons soy sauce

1 tablespoon rice wine vinegar

1 tablespoon honey

1 teaspoon toasted sesame seeds

Waloumi (Waffled Haloumi Cheese) and Watermelon

IRON: Belgian or standard | **TIME:** 15 minutes | **YIELD:** Serves 4

Grilled cheese, anyone?

Haloumi is grilled cheese that doesn't let the bread get in the way of the cheese—because there is no bread. It's just cheese, grilled. Or waffled, technically. Haloumi's high melting point means that it maintains its shape in the waffle iron—except, of course, for taking on the distinctive divots of the waffle iron.

Serving watermelon with salt is a classic. Impart that salty quality in the form of waffled cheese and you have a quick snack or an appetizer that's a visual standout.

1   Preheat the waffle iron on medium.

2   Slice the watermelon into 8 wedges about ½ inch thick—big enough to accommodate a piece of waffled cheese stacked atop them. Trim off the rind if you'd like, or leave it on to add a splash of color to the dish. Set the watermelon wedges aside.

3   Place the cheese slices on the waffle iron and close the lid.

4   Cook for 2 minutes before checking. The cheese is ready when it has waffle marks and turns golden brown in most spots.

5   To serve, stack a piece of waffled cheese atop each watermelon wedge and drizzle with olive oil. Sprinkle with salt and pepper to taste.

INGREDIENTS

8 ounces haloumi, cut into 8 slices

Small seedless watermelon

Extra-virgin olive oil, for drizzling

Salt and freshly ground black pepper, to taste

TIP

Juustoleipä is a Finnish cheese with similar characteristics to haloumi and can be substituted in this recipe.

Cheesy Waffled Arancini

IRON: Belgian or standard | **TIME:** 30 minutes | **YIELD:** Makes 8 arancini; serves 4

The crunchy exterior wraps up a cheesy, melty interior.

INGREDIENTS

2 cups cooked short-grain white rice such as Arborio, prepared according to package directions and cooled

½ cup grated Parmesan cheese

¼ teaspoon salt

¼ teaspoon freshly ground black pepper

3 large eggs

2 ounces fresh mozzarella, cut into 8 chunks

1 cup seasoned bread crumbs (see Tip, page 144)

Nonstick cooking spray

1 cup marinara sauce (see Spaghetti and Waffled Meatballs, Steps 1 to 5, page 65)

Traditionally, arancini are fried balls of rice with a crunchy exterior that hides a little surprise inside. When they're made in the waffle iron, the surprise is outside *and* inside.

This recipe gives new life to leftover rice—but it's good enough that it's worth making rice for the occasion. If you make the rice for this dish, you'll need to allow a few hours for it to cool in the refrigerator before you proceed with the recipe below.

1 Preheat the waffle iron on medium. Preheat the oven on its lowest setting.

2 In a medium-size bowl, combine the rice, Parmesan, salt, pepper, and 1 of the eggs, and stir to thoroughly blend.

3 With wet hands, form each rice ball by taking a small portion of the mixture, squeezing it firmly into a ball, and stuffing a chunk of mozzarella inside the ball. The cheese should be completely encased in the rice.

Repeat this process to form 8 arancini balls and set them aside.

4 Whisk together the remaining 2 eggs in a small bowl. Set the bread crumbs in a shallow bowl or deep dish, such as a pie pan. Dip each of the arancini in the egg mixture and then in the bread crumbs, shaking off any excess. Handle the arancini delicately. (Don't worry too much, though—if one falls apart, just press it back together.)

5 Coat both sides of the waffle iron grid with nonstick spray. Place a ball of arancini in each section of the waffle iron, close the lid, and cook until the arancini hold together as a cohesive unit, 4 minutes. (Some cheese may start to escape by the time they're ready to remove.)

6 While the arancini are cooking, heat the marinara sauce in the microwave for 45 seconds, or in a small saucepan on the stovetop over low heat.

7 Remove the arancini from the waffle iron and repeat Steps 5 and 6 with the remaining arancini. Keep the finished arancini warm in the oven.

8 Serve arancini with the warm marinara sauce.

TIP

If you want to make your own seasoned bread crumbs, combine a scant cup of plain bread crumbs with 2 tablespoons of Italian seasoning mix, or 1 teaspoon each of dried parsley flakes, garlic powder, onion powder, dried oregano, and sugar.

Zucchini-Parmesan Flattened Fritters

IRON: Belgian or standard | **TIME:** 40 minutes, including 30 minutes of draining time for zucchini | **YIELD:** Serves 4

If you're looking to add some zip to your vegetables, look no further.

At the peak of summer, zucchini grows like a weed in certain gardens. Disguising the squash and foisting it on unsuspecting (or, in my case, suspecting) friends and relatives becomes a mealtime game.

Enter the waffle iron. Even jaded, zucchini-weary diners will eagerly scarf down a few of these fritters. They come together quickly, too.

Squeezing some of the excess moisture from the zucchini makes for a denser final product that holds together better. Don't skip this step, but, if you're in a hurry, you can cut the time in half.

1 Place the zucchini in a strainer or colander and sprinkle with ¼ teaspoon of the salt. Let it stand for 30 minutes. Rinse well with cold water. Press to remove excess liquid from the zucchini and then blot dry with a clean lint-free towel or paper towels.

2 Preheat the waffle iron on medium. Preheat the oven on its lowest setting.

3 In a large bowl, whisk the egg and then add the milk and ¼ cup of the Parmesan. Whisk well to combine.

INGREDIENTS

2 cups shredded zucchini (about 2 medium-size zucchini)

½ teaspoon salt

1 large egg

¼ cup milk

½ cup grated Parmesan cheese

½ cup all-purpose flour

¼ teaspoon freshly ground black pepper

Nonstick cooking spray

4 In a small bowl, combine the flour, remaining ¼ teaspoon salt, and pepper. Mix well and stir into the large bowl with the egg mixture. Add the zucchini and toss until well combined.

5 Coat both sides of the waffle iron grid with nonstick spray. Place rounded tablespoons of the zucchini mixture on the waffle iron, leaving space between each scoop for the fritters to spread. Close the lid.

6 Cook until lightly browned and cooked through, 3 minutes, and remove from the waffle iron.

7 Repeat Steps 5 and 6 with remaining batter. Keep the finished fritters warm in the oven.

8 To serve, top the fritters with the remaining ¼ cup Parmesan.

VARIATIONS

- Substitute finely chopped broccoli or shredded carrot for the zucchini. (It's not necessary to drain these.)
- Substitute an equal amount of grated Cheddar or Asiago for the Parmesan.
- Add ½ teaspoon onion or garlic powder in Step 4 with the salt and pepper.

Waffled Tostones

| **IRON:** Belgian or standard (with a Belgian-style iron, tostones will have to be arranged on the grid for the maximum number of waffle marks) | **TIME:** 30 minutes | **YIELD:** Serves 4 |

(It's pronounced "toast-OWN-ays.")

INGREDIENTS

2 quarts neutral-flavored oil, such as canola, for frying

2 yellow plantains (a little bit of green is fine)

Salt, to taste

Garlic Dipping Sauce (recipe follows)

If there's any food that's a match for the waffle iron, it's something where the traditional recipe calls for it to be smashed.

Meet tostones.

Tostones are made from plantains—those slightly exotic relatives of bananas. The aroma and taste of many plantains suggest the sweet banana with which you may be most familiar, but with less sweetness. Green plantains are the most starchy and potato-like, while yellow ones have a little more sweetness. Either is fine, but be aware that green ones will take longer both to fry and to waffle.

This Latin American dish is sometimes fried with garlic, but this version keeps them plain and then adds a garlic dipping sauce. Typical tostones may be cut thicker, but ¾ inch and ½ inch were too thick for satisfactory waffling. Better to go with something thinner, like the ¼-inch cut used here.

Waffled tostones pair perfectly with a Waffled Cuban Sandwich (page 44).

1 Pour the oil into a large pot or Dutch oven, taking care to leave plenty of room at the top of the pot. The oil must not come up more than halfway, or it could bubble over when the plantains are added.

2 Bring the oil to 350°F on an instant-read thermometer over medium heat.

3 While the oil heats, peel the plantains. Slice off each end and then cut 3 slits lengthwise along

the plantain. Pry the skin off with your fingers. Cut each plantain into slices about ¼ inch thick.

4 Preheat the waffle iron on medium. Warm a platter in the oven on its lowest setting.

5 When the oil reaches about 350°F, a cube of bread dropped into the oil will turn light brown in 60 seconds. Fry the plantain slices at this temperature for 1 minute.

6 After a minute, check a plantain slice to see if it's done. It should be a light golden color and cooked on the outside. The more green the plantain is, the longer it will take to fry—up to about 3 minutes.

7 With a slotted spoon, remove the fried plantains from the oil and drain on a plate lined with paper towels. A little oil clinging

to them is fine—in fact, it will help when they go into the waffle iron.

8 Place as many fried plantains as will fit in a single layer on the waffle iron, leaving a bit of room for them to expand.

9 Press the cover of the waffle iron down to smash the plantains flat. Careful: The lid may be hot.

10 Cook until the plantains are a deep golden brown and are soft throughout, 2 minutes.

11 Remove the plantains from the waffle iron. Repeat Steps 8 through 10 with the remaining plantains.

12 Place finished plantains on a warm platter, and sprinkle with salt. Serve with the Garlic Dipping Sauce.

INGREDIENTS

2 cloves garlic, unpeeled

¼ cup extra-virgin olive oil

1 large handful cilantro, large stems removed, finely chopped

Salt, to taste

Garlic Dipping Sauce

1 Smash the garlic cloves with the heel of your hand and peel the garlic. Add the garlic to the olive oil in a small bowl. Stir in the chopped cilantro.

2 Let the mixture sit for 10 minutes. Remove the garlic cloves and discard them.

3 Add a pinch of salt and taste to see if it needs more.

Waffled Fries

IRON: Belgian or standard | **TIME:** 10 minutes | **YIELD:** Serves 4

I could eat these in quantities I am not quite willing to admit.

Waffle fries already exist, so the question wasn't how to invent waffle fries, but how to reinvent them as *waffled* fries.

Previous experimentation with hash browns suggested a few things. First, cooking raw potatoes in the waffle iron is only going to work if the potatoes are very thinly sliced—but that's not what we're looking for.

So I went into this recipe knowing I would start with cooked potatoes. But how would they be cooked? I tried partially baking the potatoes in the oven and then waffling them. This resulted in a potato that had too much resistance, a potato so sturdy that it barely registered the waffle indentations. Next, I tried potatoes that had been fully baked and cooled only slightly. These yielded to the grid of the waffle iron, but they mostly tasted and looked like baked potato that had been cooked in the waffle iron.

What I needed was something that would get crispy on the outside and stay slightly moist—but not mushy—on the inside.

My thoughts turned to those mashed potatoes from a box.

Traditional mashed potatoes would be too moist. So I added less water than the package directions called for. Success. I was on to something. But they still weren't as crisp and brown as I would have liked. I added some butter. A little more tinkering with the potato-to-water ratio and voilà! The direct heat of the waffle iron leaves the exterior of the waffled fry crispy, and the slightly moist, potatoey inside is remarkably reminiscent of a perfectly cooked French fry.

1 Preheat the waffle iron on high. Coat both sides of the waffle iron grid with nonstick spray.

2 Combine the melted butter, water, and salt in a bowl. Add the potato flakes and stir the mixture thoroughly. Allow it to sit while the waffle iron comes to the desired temperature. The mixture will be quite thick.

3 For each waffled fry, put about a tablespoon of potato mixture in the waffle iron. Fit as much of the potato mixture as you can on the waffle iron grid, close the lid, and cook until deep golden brown, 3 minutes. Remove the fries and repeat, spraying the waffle iron grid again if necessary, until you have used up all of the potato mixture.

4 Serve the fries with ketchup or mayonnaise.

INGREDIENTS

Nonstick cooking spray

4 tablespoons (½ stick) unsalted butter, melted

1 cup water

½ teaspoon salt

2 cups instant potato flakes

Ketchup or mayonnaise, for serving

Waffled Onion Rings

IRON: Belgian or standard | **TIME:** 20 minutes | **YIELD:** Serves 4

I'm not going to claim I spent sleepless nights contemplating waffled onion rings, but they were the subject of a lot of daydreaming.

At first, I was very literal. I pictured dipping each onion slice in batter and then setting it in the waffle iron. It seemed a little tedious. Only one or two onion rings at a time would fit in most waffle irons. I needed to figure out how to fill the waffle iron with a giant onion ring, where every bite was part onion and part crunchy

NOTE: Belgian-style irons give more room for the batter to rise and result in lighter, fluffier onion rings.

◄ **WAFFLED FRIES**

INGREDIENTS

1½ cups all-purpose flour

½ cup cornstarch

1 tablespoon baking powder

2 teaspoons salt

2 teaspoons granulated sugar

1 teaspoon freshly ground black pepper

1 teaspoon onion powder

12 ounces lager-style beer

¼ cup neutral-flavored oil, such as canola

1 large onion, thinly sliced and then cut into segments no more than 1 inch long

Nonstick cooking spray

NOTE: This is not a place to use your expensive craft beer, the one with the great flavor. Use the cheap stuff. If you're worried about the alcohol, feel free to swap it out for a nonalcoholic beer.

coating. Arranging the batter in a ring shape rather than just pouring it in the waffle iron keeps the recipe true to the idea of an "onion ring."

With my first batch of these, the batter was too thick. It made the finished product a little leaden. And I didn't have any onion powder in the mix, so the parts that were all waffled breading and no onion were a little bland. But reducing the flour and swapping some of it for cornstarch made the batter perfectly light. Adding the onion powder ensured that even if you happen to get a bite without onion, the flavor still carries through.

1 Preheat the waffle iron on medium. Preheat the oven on its lowest setting.

2 In a large bowl, combine the flour, cornstarch, baking powder, salt, sugar, pepper, and onion powder and stir to combine. Whisk in the beer. (The mixture will foam.) Stir in the oil and then the onions.

3 Coat both sides of the waffle iron grid with nonstick spray. Pour about ¼ cup of the batter onto the waffle iron in the shape of a large ring, taking note that the batter will expand as it cooks. Your ring will not be perfect, but you can use a silicone spatula to nudge some parts of the batter into shape before closing the lid.

4 Cook for 4 minutes, or until brown. Remove the onion ring from the waffle iron.

5 Repeat Steps 3 and 4 to make the rest of the onion rings. Keep finished onion rings warm in the oven.

6 Serve hot.

VARIATIONS

• Sprinkle with sharp Cheddar cheese or serve with cheese sauce for dipping.

• Add one of the following to the flour mixture in Step 2:
  • ½ teaspoon paprika
  • ¼ teaspoon dry mustard
  • Dash of freshly grated nutmeg
  • ½ teaspoon dried thyme

Stuffles (Stuffing Waffles)

IRON: Belgian or standard | **TIME:** 30 minutes | **YIELD:** Serves 4

whether from scratch or from a box, all roads lead to stuffles.

Perhaps this isn't really stuffing, because it's not cooked inside the bird. Dressing, maybe? Either way, cooking the stuffing inside the bird has fallen out of favor because of food safety concerns. By the same token, I do not recommend putting a waffle iron inside your turkey.

Lisa Futterman gets credit for this idea. We met early on in my waffling experiments, and she became a waffle iron devotee. (Next to my mother, she might be the person most excited about this cookbook.) Her version used a bit of waffle batter as a binder for the stuffing ingredients. But I am nothing if not a purist. Okay. That's not true. I am a lot of things, if not a purist. But I am also a purist. And so I was determined to find a way to make it work with just the stuffing ingredients.

You do have to make peace with the idea that the stuffles may not come out completely intact. Some will. Many, even! But if you go into it with the idea that they will all emerge camera-ready, you will come out of it with tears (and perfectly good although perhaps cosmetically imperfect stuffles). They will still be perfectly good—and can be deliciously disguised with a topping of turkey, gravy, and cranberry sauce.

If you don't have poultry seasoning on hand, substitute equal parts of dried marjoram, thyme, and savory. And if you'd rather go the instant stuffle route, mix 3 cups stuffing mix (from a 1 ounce package) with 1½ cups water and 3 tablespoons melted butter, stir, and

INGREDIENTS

1 tablespoon extra-virgin olive oil

½ cup chopped onion

½ cup chopped celery

¾ teaspoon salt

½ teaspoon freshly ground black pepper

½ teaspoon poultry seasoning

¼ teaspoon dried sage

6 cups dry bread cubes (about ½-inch square)

½ cup unsalted butter, melted

1 cup low-sodium chicken broth

Nonstick cooking spray

NOTE: Many kinds of bread will work here, including sandwich bread and baguette—alone or in combination. Cut any slightly stale pieces or ends into cubes and stash them in a zip-top bag in the freezer until you accumulate enough for this recipe. Thaw at room temperature for an hour before using.

let hydrate for ten minutes. For this method, start the recipe in Step 6. Instant stuffles will cook more quickly than the scratch variety, so check them after 3 minutes. If you're making them from scratch, the size of the bread cubes is a rough guide. Don't spend too much time with a ruler on the bread cubes. That's time you could spend waffling.

I Place the olive oil in a large skillet over medium heat. Add the onion and celery and sauté until the onion is soft and the celery is beginning to soften, about 5 minutes.

2 Add the salt, pepper, poultry seasoning, and dried sage and cook for I minute more to heat through. Remove the pan from the heat.

3 Place the bread cubes in a large bowl. In a small bowl, whisk together the butter and chicken broth, then pour that mixture over the bread. Add the vegetable mixture and stir.

4 Preheat the waffle iron on medium. Preheat the oven on its lowest setting.

5 Allow the stuffing mixture to sit for 5 minutes to absorb the liquid completely, stirring it once or twice.

6 Coat both sides of the waffle iron grid with nonstick spray.

Measure about ½ cup of the stuffing mix and place it on one section of the waffle iron. (This measure is approximate. Use enough of the mixture to slightly overstuff each section of the waffle iron. Waffle irons with deeper grooves may need a bit more stuffing.)

7 Close the lid and press down to compress the stuffing.

8 After 4 minutes, open the lid to check on the stuffle. It should be golden brown and cohesive. Use a silicone spatula to loosen the edges before sliding the spatula underneath the stuffle and lifting it out. (If you're worried about the stuffle holding together, it may be easier to use two spatulas—one for the top and one for the bottom.)

9 Repeat Steps 6 through 8 for the remaining stuffing mixture. Keep completed stuffles warm in the oven.

Chapter 5
Desserts

Waffled Pineapple
Dusted with Chili Powder

IRON: Belgian or standard | **TIME:** 15 minutes | **YIELD:** Serves 4 (based on 20-ounce can of pineapple; servings from fresh fruit will depend on size)

Serve this with cottage cheese or plain Greek yogurt—the perfect complement to sweet and spicy.

Fruit on the grill reminds me of summer. The natural sugars in the fruit caramelize beautifully and the flavors intensify. But it can't always be summer. And you can't always have a grill. So why not put fruit on the waffle iron?

Chili powder on fruit is a Mexican favorite—mango dusted with the dark red spice is a classic example. The bright smokiness of the chili cuts the sweetness of the fruit.

Fresh pineapple is available year-round, but the price can vary and the convenience of the canned version can't be beat. So I tried both fresh and canned. Here are the pros and cons:

The fresh is clearly more labor-intensive. The results are slightly superior if you like a little bit of resistance when you bite into it.

The canned version saves time and labor. Because the pineapple has already been heated in the canning process before it goes into the waffle iron, it is essentially being cooked twice, so the resulting waffled pineapple is a bit softer. But because even the fresh pineapple softens significantly when it's waffled, the result is not wildly different.

INGREDIENTS

Nonstick cooking spray

1 whole pineapple or
  1 (20 ounce) can of
  pineapple

Chili powder

One thing to consider: The center of a pineapple has a fibrous, almost woody core. The canned variety has this conveniently removed, but what about the fresh pineapple? Is it worth removing it? You can if you wish. But the good news is that if you keep the slices of the fresh pineapple thin, that core will soften significantly while it waffles. It's probably not worth the trouble of removing it.

I Preheat the waffle iron on medium. Coat both sides of the waffle iron grid with nonstick spray.

2 **FOR FRESH PINEAPPLE:** Lay the pineapple on its side and cut off the crown and the bottom of the pineapple to give you two flat ends. Stand the pineapple upright and trim off the sides of the pineapple, starting with your knife at the top and working your way down. A few pieces of skin may remain. Use a small spoon to remove them. Turn the pineapple on its side and make even slices about ½ inch thick. If the slices are thicker than ½ inch, the waffle iron may not be able to press down evenly across the fruit.

FOR CANNED PINEAPPLE: Open the can and drain the juice from the fruit. Set the sliced pineapple on a plate covered with paper towels and blot the slices dry. You want as little residual liquid remaining as possible, because the juice can burn in the waffle iron.

3 Place the slices of pineapple on the waffle iron grid and close the lid. For fresh pineapple, cook for 4 minutes before checking. For canned pineapple, cook for I minute before checking. When the pineapple is starting to show golden brown waffle indentations, remove it and place it on a platter.

4 Dust the pineapple with chili powder and serve.

VARIATIONS

• Instead of chili powder, dust the pineapple with ground ginger.

• Skip the chili powder and top the pineapple with crushed macadamia nuts.

Waffled Oatmeal Chocolate Chip Cookies

IRON: Belgian or standard | **TIME:** 45 minutes | **YIELD:** Makes about 20 cookies

The portability of the waffle iron is key here: You can churn out warm cookies from anywhere with a working outlet.

Your brain reads waffle, but your taste buds say cookie. And they're both right.

If you only have regular chocolate chips on hand, don't let that stop you from making these cookies. But if you're going shopping for ingredients, you should pick up the mini chocolate chips.

Testing with standard-size chips worked most of the time, except when a few chips poked out of the dough and came into direct contact with the heat of the waffle iron. Those cookies had black streaks of slightly burnt chocolate on the exteriors. They were delicious but not as pretty as the ones with mini chips, and not as consistent.

Don't make the cookies too big. They have to be removed from the waffle iron while they're still fairly soft. Anything bigger than a heaping tablespoon of batter will tend to yield cookies that become unwieldy and fall apart as you attempt to remove them.

Yes, this is an excuse to eat the broken ones. But you don't want them all to be broken.

Right?

1 Preheat the waffle iron on medium.

2 In a large bowl, beat the butter and brown sugar with an electric hand mixer until mostly smooth.

3 Add the eggs and vanilla, then continue beating until they're fully incorporated.

4 In a medium-size bowl, combine the flour, baking soda, and salt. Add these dry ingredients to the wet ingredients and mix until few streaks of flour remain.

5 Add the oats and chocolate chips and stir to combine.

6 Coat both sides of the waffle iron grid with nonstick spray.

7 Place a heaping tablespoon of dough onto each waffle section, allowing room for the cookies to spread. Close the lid and cook until the cookies are set and beginning to brown. This won't take very long—2 or 3 minutes, depending on the heat of your waffle iron. The cookies should be soft when you remove them and will firm up as they cool.

8 Transfer the cookies to a wire rack to cool.

9 Repeat Steps 6 through 8 until the remaining batter has been waffled.

INGREDIENTS

½ cup unsalted butter, softened

½ cup firmly packed light brown sugar

2 large eggs

1 teaspoon pure vanilla extract

½ cup all-purpose flour

½ teaspoon baking soda

¼ teaspoon salt

¾ cup old-fashioned rolled oats

¾ cup semisweet mini chocolate chips

Nonstick cooking spray

NOTE: You can substitute the all-purpose flour with an equal amount of white whole wheat flour. This may make the cookies cook more quickly, so keep an eye on them.

TIPS

• To expedite the cooking, try this: While one batch is on the waffle iron, scoop up heaping tablespoons of dough and set these portions along one side of the bowl's interior. When one batch is finished, recoat the waffle iron with nonstick spray, plop the measured balls of dough onto the grid, and cook.

• To freeze the cookie dough: Form the dough into balls, place them on a tray to freeze and then, once frozen, place the balls of dough into a zip-top bag. The frozen dough can go right onto the waffle iron (just add another minute to the cook time).

Waffled Mochi
with Green Tea Ice Cream

IRON: Belgian or standard (a Belgian-style iron provides the most room for the mochi to expand and reach its light, airy potential)	**TIME:** 20 minutes	**YIELD:** Serves 4

Although bland on its own, mochi becomes the perfect canvas for layering flavors.

Mochi is Japanese rice made into a paste and formed into sheets. It's wonderfully malleable, both in texture and in taste. I would like to claim that this recipe simply came to me. But the reality is that much of this recipe came to me from Japan—in a suitcase. There's a bit of a story behind this one.

When my friend Stu and his girlfriend, Yoshimi, came from Japan to visit, she brought a suitcase full of food. It was as if she was unaware that we had supermarkets here, too. Stu and I watched as she unpacked onto my kitchen counter: From her suitcase emerged five packages of rice, curry sauce, a shelf-stable plastic package of cooked corn, several bags of candy, jars of condiments—and mochi. Those are just the items I could halfway identify. Most of them I couldn't.

She was in town a few days before we waffled. The night before the morning in question, she went out to buy cheese and tomato sauce. She had big plans.

That morning, we made waffled pizza mochi, laying strips of cheese and a thin layer of sauce between slices of mochi and then piling the assembled stack into the waffle iron.

INGREDIENTS

Nonstick cooking spray

4 strips mochi, each about
2 inches by 3 inches and
⅛ inch thick

1 pint green tea ice cream

1 ounce candied mango,
cut into thin strips

TIP

Candied fruit can be sticky.
To make clean slices, coat
your knife with a very thin
layer of oil. Dab some
neutral-flavored oil (such
as canola) on a paper
towel, then wipe the blade
against the paper towel.

We closed the lid and waited. There's always that moment where you don't know what's happening inside. Maybe it gurgles softly. Maybe wisps of steam puff out. But you can't peek—not for a few minutes, anyway.

Then it was time to look.

The pizza mochi came out like a giant puffed rice cake with cheese and sauce—bubbly and melty and delicious. Thin, flat strips of mochi tripled or quadrupled in height. Perhaps we were on to something.

We ate our first experiment as we forged ahead. Up next: plain waffled mochi, topped with vanilla ice cream, and drizzled with a Japanese-style molasses and sweet bean powder.

We were no longer surprised it worked—just delighted.

A few days later, Yoshimi headed back to Japan.

She left me a package of mochi.

It seems wrong to require a Japanese houseguest and a suitcase full of ingredients as a prerequisite for a recipe. So I went back to the drawing board to come up with this. Green tea ice cream, mochi, and candied mango are available at some health food stores and Asian supermarkets, but also at regular supermarkets that cater to more adventurous eaters.

1 Preheat the waffle iron on medium. Coat both sides of the waffle iron grid with nonstick spray.

2 Set a strip of mochi on each section of the waffle iron.

3 Close the lid and cook the mochi until it's puffy, about 3 minutes.

4 Remove the mochi, and place it on a cutting board to cool.

5 Put a piece of mochi on each plate and top each piece with a small scoop of ice cream. (To make compact balls of ice cream, use 2 spoons to mold them into shape.)

6 Arrange the mango slices on top of the ice cream and serve.

VARIATIONS

Mochi is a great canvas, making this recipe very flexible.
As variations, consider these combinations:

- Blood orange sorbet + candied ginger
- Banana ice cream + toasted sesame seeds
- Mango sorbet + crushed macadamia nuts
- Vanilla ice cream + chocolate chips
- Peanut butter ice cream + grape jelly
- Peach ice cream + slivered almonds

Red Velvet Waffle Ice Cream Sandwiches

| **IRON:** Belgian or standard (see Tip on page 172 regarding preparation in Belgian-style iron) | **TIME:** 2 hours (includes I hour for allowing sandwiches to freeze) | **YIELD:** Makes 8 sandwiches |

Testing this recipe was brutal: I can't tell you how many "failures" I had to eat.

You're not going to have to try very hard to make these look and taste amazing.

I would pat myself on the back for all the iterations I tried to perfect this recipe except that—let's be honest—what we're really talking about is me eating ice cream sandwiches. It's not exactly digging ditches.

With a typical ice cream sandwich, the cookie part is fragile enough that it pays to assemble them carefully by cutting sandwich-size slices from a sheet of ice cream that has been softened and then refrozen in the perfect shape. With waffling, we can forget all that. The waffle cookies are sturdy enough to withstand a little spatula action. Just spread the softened ice cream right on there.

The classic vanilla ice cream on red velvet waffle cookies is a winner. But you can try other flavors, too. See page 172 for suggestions.

INGREDIENTS

1¾ cups all-purpose flour

¼ cup unsweetened cocoa

1 teaspoon baking soda

1 teaspoon salt

1 cup canola oil

1 cup granulated sugar

1 large egg

3 tablespoons red food coloring

1 teaspoon pure vanilla extract

1½ teaspoons distilled white vinegar

½ cup buttermilk

Nonstick cooking spray

1½ quarts vanilla ice cream

2 cups semisweet mini chocolate chips

NOTE: One difference between premium ice creams and less expensive versions is the amount of air incorporated into the ice cream. This makes a difference when it comes to making these sandwiches: The cheaper ice cream will tend to be fluffier, will soften more quickly, and will be easier to spread.

1 Preheat the waffle iron on medium.

2 In a medium-size bowl, whisk together the flour, cocoa, baking soda, and salt. Set aside.

3 In the bowl of a stand mixer, or with an electric hand mixer in a large bowl, beat the oil and sugar at medium speed until well blended. Beat in the egg. Turn down the mixer to low, and slowly add the food coloring and vanilla.

4 Mix the vinegar and the buttermilk together. Add half of this buttermilk mixture to the large bowl with the oil, sugar, and egg. Stir to combine, and then add half of the flour mixture. Scrape down the bowl and stir only enough to make sure there is no unmixed flour. Add the rest of the buttermilk mixture, stir to combine, and then add the last of the flour mixture. Stir again, just enough to make sure there is no unmixed flour.

5 Coat both sides of the waffle iron grid with nonstick spray. Pour enough batter into the waffle iron to cover the grid, close the lid, and cook until the waffles are firm enough to remove from the waffle iron, 4 minutes.

6 Allow the waffles to cool slightly on a wire rack. Use kitchen shears or a sharp knife to separate the waffles into sections (probably rectangles, wedges, or hearts, depending on your waffle iron). Repeat to make a total of 16 sections.

7 While the waffle sections are cooling, set the ice cream on the counter to soften for 10 minutes.

8 After the ice cream has softened, set out half of the waffle sections and use a spatula to spread ice cream about 1 inch thick on each of them. Top with the remaining sections to make 8 sandwiches. Scrape off any ice cream overflow with a rubber

spatula to neaten the edges. Then dunk the edges of the ice cream into a bowl or shallow dish filled with mini chocolate chips.

9 Wrap each sandwich tightly in plastic wrap, place in a zip-top bag, and place the bag in the freezer for at least 1 hour to allow the ice cream to harden. Remove a sandwich a few minutes before serving to allow it to soften slightly.

VARIATIONS

- Use cookies-and-cream ice cream for a filling, with the edges dunked in crushed chocolate sandwich cookies.

- Use chocolate ice cream and dunk the edges in crushed peanuts instead of mini chocolate chips.

Waffled Banana Bread

| **IRON:** Belgian or standard | **TIME:** 45 minutes | **YIELD:** Makes 10 to 15 waffled banana bread slices |

Use bananas as ripe as you'd want to eat—save the mushy ones for conventional banana bread.

The first time I made this, we were having guests for brunch. They texted before they came over. "Should we bring anything? Croissants? Fruit?"

I looked at the mess on my counter. Was it fair to subject them to my waffling experiments?

INGREDIENTS

1 cup plus 2 tablespoons granulated sugar

1 teaspoon ground cinnamon

3 medium-size ripe bananas, sliced into ⅛-inch-thick rounds

8 tablespoons (1 stick) unsalted butter, softened

½ cup packed light brown sugar

6 ounces cream cheese, softened, cut into approximately 1-ounce chunks

2 large eggs

1 teaspoon pure vanilla extract

1½ cups all-purpose flour

½ cup uncooked old-fashioned oats

1½ teaspoons baking powder

¼ teaspoon salt

Nonstick cooking spray

NOTE: Slicing the bananas thinly means the finished product doesn't have chunks of banana. What it does have is banana flavor melted throughout.

"Bring both!" I told them. At worst, we'd have leftovers. At best, I wouldn't have to subject them to a failed experiment.

I didn't want to be too needy. ("They're great, aren't they?") I watched everyone's reaction carefully. One serving was polite. Two helpings was encouraging. A third trip was convincing. It turns out, I didn't have to worry: They were a hit.

There were two pieces left over. Those got tossed in the freezer. A day later, they were gone, too.

1 In a small bowl, mix 2 tablespoons of the granulated sugar and the cinnamon. Place the sliced banana pieces in a small bowl, then sprinkle them with the cinnamon-sugar mixture. Stir to distribute the cinnamon-sugar mixture evenly. Let the bananas stand for 30 minutes.

2 In the bowl of a stand mixer fitted with the paddle attachment or with an electric hand mixer, mix the butter, the remaining cup of granulated sugar, and brown sugar until well blended. Add the cream cheese and mix until it is completely incorporated into the sugar mixture. Add the eggs one at a time and mix until they are just blended into the batter. Add the vanilla and mix well to combine.

3 In a medium-size mixing bowl, combine the flour, oats, baking powder, and salt. Once combined, pour the flour mixture into the butter and sugar mixture. Mix until the dry ingredients are completely blended into the wet ingredients, scraping down the bowl to make sure the mixture is thoroughly combined.

4 Pour the bananas and any accumulated liquid into the bowl, and fold gently to incorporate.

5 Preheat the waffle iron on medium. Coat both sides of the waffle iron grid with nonstick spray. Preheat the oven on its lowest setting.

6 Coat the inside of a ⅓ cup measuring cup with nonstick spray to help release the batter. Measure out ⅓ cup of batter and pour onto the preheated waffle iron. Close the lid and cook until the banana bread is dark golden brown, 5 minutes. (If you lift it out of the waffle iron too soon, it won't hold together.)

7 Remove the finished piece from the waffle iron and place it on a wire rack to cool slightly. Repeat Step 6 with the remaining batter. Keep finished pieces warm in the oven.

8 Serve warm or at room temperature.

Wapple Pie
(Waffled Apple Pie)

IRON: Belgian (standard irons may not produce a deep enough waffle to split the "pie" into a top and bottom crust, but see the Tip on page 178 for an easy alternative)	**TIME:** 1 hour	**YIELD:** Makes 4 pies

The quintessential American dessert gets an assist from a French pastry.

For this recipe, I needed something that would accommodate the apple pie filling. I wanted a top and bottom crust, but nothing too dense.

Pâte à choux batter is what is typically used for éclairs—those light pastries with room for cream or chocolate. When the dough hits the heat, it puffs up and leaves pockets of air. That is, it does when it's cooked in the oven. The question was how it would work in the waffle iron.

Chicago pastry chef Meg Galus encouraged me to try it. I didn't need much convincing.

First I made the filling. I prefer tart apples with just a touch of sweetness. If you'd like a sweeter filling, add another tablespoon of sugar.

Then I took a stab at the crust.

The pâte à choux puffs up in the waffle iron and leaves some pockets. Cutting open the waffled pâte à choux reveals a space for the filling.

A little dusting of cinnamon, a little whipped cream or ice cream, and you're set.

1 Make the filling: Peel and core the apples. Cut into ¼- to ½-inch-thick dice.

2 In a medium-size saucepan, combine the apples with the remaining filling ingredients and cover. Cook over medium-low heat, stirring occasionally. Reduce the heat if the apples start to scorch. Continue cooking until the apples soften, about 10 minutes. (If the apples show no sign of softening, add a teaspoon of water, continue cooking, and check after 5 minutes more. Repeat with another teaspoon of water and another 5 minutes of cooking, if necessary.)

3 Taste and adjust the seasoning as necessary. Sweeter apples may benefit from a bit more lemon juice. Apples on the tart side may require more sugar. Set aside.

4 Make the crust: In a small saucepan, bring the water, butter, salt, and sugar to a simmer over high heat.

5 When the butter has melted and the sugar and salt have dissolved, lower the heat to medium, add the flour, and stir rapidly. The dough will form quickly as the flour absorbs the water mixture. Continue to cook over medium heat for 1 minute.

6 Remove the saucepan from the heat and allow the mixture to stand for 5 minutes. When it has cooled slightly, add the eggs one at a time, stirring until each is combined into the batter. The batter will be very stiff and look a bit like buttercream frosting.

7 Preheat the waffle iron on medium-high. Coat both sides of the waffle iron grid with nonstick spray.

8 Place about ¼ cup of the batter on one section of the waffle iron. Close the lid and cook until it is thoroughly brown, 5 to 10 minutes. If your waffle iron makes thicker waffles, you may have to cut into it to check if it is cooked through. (This is okay because you'll be cutting into the crust anyway to stuff it.) Repeat with the remaining batter.

INGREDIENTS

-3 medium-size Granny Smith or similarly tart apples such as Northern Spy, Jonathan, or Pippin

2 tablespoons granulated sugar

1 tablespoon unsalted butter

1 tablespoon all-purpose flour

1 teaspoon lemon juice

¼ teaspoon ground cinnamon

Pinch of ground nutmeg

Pinch of salt

Crust:

½ cup water

4 tablespoons (½ stick) unsalted butter

¼ teaspoon salt

2 teaspoons granulated sugar

½ cup all-purpose flour

2 large eggs

Nonstick cooking spray

Ground cinnamon, for dusting (optional)

Whipped cream or vanilla ice cream, for serving

9 With a sharp knife, create a pocket for the filling by cutting from one corner of the waffled crust almost to the other edge, without cutting through all the way. (You want a wedge with a hinge on one side.)

10 Spoon about ¼ cup of the pie filling into the pocket.

11 To serve, dust with cinnamon, if desired, and top with whipped cream or vanilla ice cream.

TIPS

- Crunched for time? Prepared apple pie filling is often available canned in the baking aisle of the supermarket.

- Like your pie with Cheddar? Sprinkle a bit of shredded cheese on top of the crust just before it's ready to come out of the waffle iron. The cheese should take 15 to 30 seconds to melt.

- Want a streamlined version? Working with a standard waffle iron? Skip creating a pocket in the waffled crust and just top it with the filling.

S'moreffles
(Waffled S'mores)

IRON: Belgian or standard (see instructions for creating open-face s'moreffles with a Belgian-style iron)	**TIME:** 30 minutes	**YIELD:** Serves 4

A true testament to determination, perseverance, and marshmallows.

S'moreffles are the best idea I never had.

Onetime chocolatier and all-the-time genius Lauren Pett gets the credit for this one, both for the idea of s'mores in the waffle iron and for the ingenious, Muppet-like name.

Lauren owned a chocolate shop when I came to her with the ridiculous idea of making things in the waffle iron. It didn't take long for her to settle on s'moreffles. Mind you, neither of us knew how this would work. We just knew that it had to.

Our first try was a mess. Don't put the chocolate and the marshmallows in with the batter at the same time. Chocolate and marshmallows that have been in the waffle iron for 3 minutes are not pretty.

But we picked ourselves up, cleaned off the waffle iron, and realized it would have to be a two-part process. First, the waffled graham cracker gets cooked. Then the chocolate and marshmallow get warmed just enough to melt.

1 Preheat the waffle iron on medium. Coat both sides of the waffle iron grid with nonstick spray.

2 In a mixing bowl, combine the flours, brown sugar, baking soda, salt, and cinnamon. In a separate bowl, whisk together the melted butter, milk, honey, and vanilla.

3 Add the wet ingredients to the flour mixture and stir until a dough forms.

4 Let the mixture stand for 5 minutes. It will be much thicker than ordinary waffle batter, but not as thick as bread dough.

5 Measure out about ¼ cup of batter and place it on one section of the waffle iron. Repeat with another ¼ cup of batter, to give you a top and a bottom for your s'moreffle sandwich.

6 Close the lid and cook until the waffled graham crackers are still slightly soft but cooked throughout, 3 minutes.

7 Carefully remove the waffled graham crackers from the waffle iron. They will be quite soft, so use care to keep them intact. Allow them to cool slightly. Repeat Steps 5 to 7 with the rest of the batter.

ASSEMBLY, STANDARD WAFFLE IRON:

1 Top one waffled graham cracker with a layer of chocolate chips and another with a layer of marshmallows, leaving room toward the edge for the chocolate and marshmallow to melt and spread outward.

2 Allow each waffled graham cracker to sit for a minute and the toppings to melt slightly, then press the marshmallow or chocolate into each waffle with the back of a fork. This will help you assemble the pieces.

3 Sandwich the two pieces together and place the s'moreffle in the waffle iron on the side farthest from the hinge.

4 Close the waffle iron, and allow the heat to melt the chocolate and the marshmallows, about 1 minute. Remove the s'moreffle.

5 Repeat Steps 1 to 4 for the remaining s'moreffle. Slice in half and serve.

ASSEMBLY, BELGIAN WAFFLE IRON:

1 Top one waffled graham cracker with a layer of chocolate chips and marshmallows, leaving room at the edge for the chocolate and marshmallow to melt and spread outward.

INGREDIENTS

Nonstick cooking spray

½ cup white whole wheat flour

½ cup all-purpose flour

¼ cup firmly packed dark brown sugar

½ teaspoon baking soda

¼ teaspoon salt

Pinch of ground cinnamon

4 tablespoons (½ stick) unsalted butter, melted

2 tablespoons milk

¼ cup honey

1 tablespoon pure vanilla extract

¾ cup semisweet chocolate chips

¾ cup mini marshmallows

NOTE: White whole wheat flour is a lighter, softer version of regular whole wheat flour, and if you have it, use it. The slightly nutty flavor of the whole wheat comes through in the final version and really delivers the graham cracker taste. You may, in a pinch, use just all-purpose flour—it will be fine. But don't substitute all whole wheat flour, or the result will be too dense.

TIP

To measure honey more easily, first spray the measuring cup with nonstick spray or wipe the inside with a paper towel dabbed with oil.

2 Place the s'moreffle on the waffle iron and bring the lid down so that it hovers about 1 inch above the marshmallow. Do not let the lid touch the marshmallow or chocolate. Hold for 1 minute, or until the chocolate and marshmallow are melted. Remove the open-faced s'moreffle.

3 Repeat Steps 1 and 2 for the remaining s'moreffle. Slice in half and serve.

VARIATIONS

- Substitute a thin layer of Nutella for the chocolate chips.
- Substitute a thin layer of peanut or almond butter for the marshmallows.
- Add a few grains of coarse sea salt with the chocolate chips.
- Add a drizzle of caramel sauce to the finished s'moreffle.

Chapter 6
Waffles

Yeast-Risen Overnight Waffles

IRON: Belgian or standard | **TIME:** 20 minutes, plus an hour rise on the counter and an overnight rise in the refrigerator | **YIELD:** 4 to 6 waffles; serves 4

Waffles—those other things that you can make in your waffle iron.

Would you believe that a lot of people ask me for my favorite waffle recipe? Yes, even though we *know* that waffle batter will waffle, some people seem committed to waffling waffle batter.

It takes all kinds.

My favorite waffle recipe does not require more work than other waffle recipes, but it does require that you think ahead. I know that would seem to be asking a lot sometimes, but it's not as difficult as it sounds.

Ask yourself Saturday night whether you would like delicious waffles on Sunday morning. When the answer is yes (i.e., most of the time), take 5 minutes to get these started. You can look at it as a recipe that requires thinking ahead, or you can look at it as a recipe that doesn't require much work in the morning, because most of the work will already have been done the night before.

NOTE: Some versions of overnight waffles require the mixture to stay on the counter at room temperature. But overnight refrigeration removes any food safety concerns from leaving it out at room temperature and allows a long, slow rise to contribute to the flavor of the waffle.

INGREDIENTS

2 cups all-purpose flour

1 tablespoon granulated
sugar

½ teaspoon salt

½ teaspoon instant yeast

2 cups warm milk
(about 100°F)

½ cup unsalted butter,
melted and cooled to room
temperature

1 teaspoon pure vanilla
extract

Nonstick cooking spray

2 large eggs, separated

Butter and maple syrup,
for serving

NOTE: Warming the milk
gives the yeast a head
start. Be careful not to
make it too hot, though,
or the yeast will die and the
batter won't bubble.

Now, some people to whom I have recommended this waffle recipe over the years have reported that they do not enjoy the yeasty quality of these waffles. Obviously, I disagree; I wouldn't be recommending a waffle recipe that required you to start it the night before if I didn't think it was worth it. But, yes, it's possible that you won't like them.

If that's the case, or if you fail to think ahead, there's a great buttermilk waffle recipe that follows this one.

1   In a large bowl, combine the flour, sugar, salt, and yeast. In a medium-size bowl, stir together the milk, butter, and vanilla, and then add the wet ingredients to the dry ingredients. Stir the mixture to combine thoroughly. Cover the mixture with plastic wrap or a tight-fitting lid and let it stand for an hour at room temperature before refrigerating overnight.

2   The next morning, the batter will be slightly bubbly. Preheat the waffle iron on medium and coat both sides of the waffle iron grid with nonstick spray. Preheat the oven on its lowest setting.

3   Stir the egg yolks into the batter. Place the egg whites in a medium-size bowl, and beat them until they hold soft peaks. Fold them into the batter.

4   Ladle the batter into the waffle iron and waffle until light golden brown, 3 to 5 minutes.

5   Remove the waffle. To keep it warm, place it on a wire rack in the oven. Repeat Step 4 to make the rest of the waffles.

6   Serve with butter and maple syrup.

Buttermilk Cornmeal Waffles

IRON: Belgian or standard | **TIME:** 25 minutes | **YIELD:** 4 to 6 waffles; serves 4

Buttermilk is one of those old-fashioned ingredients that deserves a place in the modern kitchen.

Here's the thing about buttermilk: You probably don't keep it on hand at all times, but you're making a mistake. It holds for a long time. What? Did you think it was going to go sour? And while there are limited applications for it, once you have it, it's easy to find excuses to use it up. So you will get the buttermilk because you want to make waffles (or pancakes) . . . and then you will make more waffles (or pancakes) because you have more buttermilk.

Buttermilk works well in this recipe because it yields slightly tangy waffles. Chances are, everything you put on the waffles will be sweet, so this recipe will bring that into balance. Even the little bit of cornmeal lends the waffles a golden hue and a slight corny flavor and crunch.

Yes, whipping the egg whites is an extra step, but it takes about 90 seconds to do and it makes a huge difference. Don't skip that part.

INGREDIENTS

1¾ cups all-purpose flour

¼ cup finely ground
    cornmeal

2 teaspoons baking soda

1 teaspoon salt

2 large eggs, separated

1¾ cups buttermilk

4 tablespoons unsalted
    butter, melted and cooled

1 teaspoon pure vanilla
    extract

Nonstick cooking spray

Butter and maple syrup,
    for serving

1 Preheat the waffle iron on medium. Preheat the oven on its lowest setting.

2 In a large bowl, whisk together the flour, cornmeal, baking soda, and salt. In a separate bowl, whisk together the egg yolks, buttermilk, butter, and vanilla.

3 In a medium-size bowl, beat the egg whites until they hold soft peaks.

4 Add the liquid ingredients to the dry ingredients while gently mixing. Then fold the egg whites into the batter.

5 Coat both sides of the waffle iron grid with nonstick spray. Pour the batter into the waffle iron, close the lid, and cook until golden brown, 3 to 5 minutes.

6 Remove the waffle. To keep it warm, place it on a wire rack in the oven. Repeat Step 5 to make the rest of the waffles.

7 Serve with butter and maple syrup.

TIP

If you enjoy having buttermilk in the house for pancakes, waffles, or waffled hamburger buns, but don't use it often enough to justify buying a quart, consider powdered buttermilk, which is available online and in the baking aisle of some grocery stores.

Appendix
Developing Your Own Waffled Recipes— and What *Won't* Waffle

Consider physics. You remember physics, right? The immutable natural laws of the universe.

Bad news: Your waffle iron cannot bend the laws of the universe. You can't let that stop you from trying new things, but you can approach your experiments prepared.

PITFALL: TOO LITTLE LIQUID

Some things—pasta and rice, for example—require a lot of moisture to cook. Spaghetti in a waffle iron is not going to work unless it's been cooked until it's al dente. Recipes like Waffled Macaroni and Cheese, page 67, and Bibimbaffle, page 111, use pasta and rice that have already been cooked and give them new life.

PITFALL: TOO MUCH LIQUID

High-moisture foods may not mesh well with the waffle iron because the trapped moisture has nowhere to go. In an oven, the dry heat provides a chance for foods to release water. The short cooking times and intense heat of the waffle iron don't always provide the same opportunity. One way around this can be to use the waffle iron as a griddle—cooking eggs with the top of the waffle iron open, for example.

PITFALL: TOO MUCH BUTTER

Butter-heavy recipes such as shortbread and tart crusts are nonstarters. Why? The intense heat of the waffle iron liquefies the butter faster than the flour can absorb it. Soon, your dreams of waffled shortbread turn into a pool of melted butter and tears.

BRINGING IT ALL TOGETHER

In general, recipes that work well fall into a few categories:

- A batter or dough that will rise and cook in the waffle iron (examples: cakes, muffins, breads)

- Components that will come together in the pressure and heat of the waffle iron (examples: hash browns, paninis)

- Solid food that will stay in one piece in the waffle iron (examples: chicken breast, steak, squid, French toast)

HOW TO SPEAK WAFFLE

So you've made your own waffle creation. As with a comet or a rain forest flower, discovery gives you naming rights. Sometimes the "waffle" can be crammed into the word itself. Exhibit A: Classic Waffleburger with Cheese. Sometimes it's a matter of mashing the "waffle" into the front or back of a word. You can see that at work with S'moreffles, Stuffles, Waloumi and Watermelon, and Wapple Pie. On the other hand, sometimes no amount of cramming can shoehorn the word into the dish name. That's when adjectives come in handy: Think *pressed, gridded, griddled, latticed, criss-crossed*—even *smashed, squished,* or *flattened.*

   With a few of my recipes, I've provided a bit of a translation in parentheses after the title. You may choose to do the same with the titles of your waffled inventions. While they may seem perfectly self-evident to you, we're not yet to the point where everyone has read this book.

THE ETYMOLOGY OF THE WORD "WAFFLE"

"Waffle" comes from the Dutch *wafel*, itself stemming from the Proto-Germanic *wabila*, meaning "web" or "honeycomb," and ultimately derived from the Proto-Indo-European root "webh," meaning "to weave." It shares history with not only "web" and "weave," but "wafer," "wave," "weevil," and "wobble."

The French word for waffle, *gaufre*, was borrowed by early 19th-century settlers to name a burrowing critter whose dens vaguely resembled a waffle's honeycomb shape, giving us "gopher."

Incidentally, waffling in the sense of blabbering—a secondary definition to the more widely used meaning, to equivocate or flip-flop—is not linguistically related to the food at all. It comes from the barking of a dog. Today they say "woof," but people in the 17th century were sure they said "waff." To waffle came to mean to yap like a dog. (Of course, in the early 21st century it acquired the meaning of cooking unexpected foods in a waffle iron.)

THE TAKEAWAY

So . . . "Is there anything that *won't* work in a waffle iron?"

I get that question a lot. I'm not sure how to answer it.

Sure, there are things that won't work in the waffle iron. Soup. Daiquiris. Ice cubes. But more than anything, this is what won't work in the waffle iron: giving up.

Some of these recipes didn't work the first time I tried them. Or the second. The ice cream sandwiches fell apart or were hard as bricks. The maple butter burned. The waffled fries were neither very waffled nor very much like fries. That's why we test recipes—again, and again, and again—to get them right.

When it comes to trying your own recipes, persevere. I've had epic meltdowns—so have my waffle irons. The only thing all of these mistakes had in common was that they did not stop me from trying again.

Conversion Tables

Please note that all conversions are approximate but close enough to be useful when converting from one system to another.

Oven Temperatures

Fahrenheit	Gas Mark	Celsius
250	½	120
275	1	140
300	2	150
325	3	160
350	4	180
375	5	190
400	6	200
425	7	220
450	8	230
475	9	240
500	10	260

NOTE: Reduce the temperature by 20°C (68°F) for fan-assisted ovens.

Approximate Equivalents

1 stick butter = 8 tbs = 4 oz = ½ cup = 115 g

1 cup all-purpose presifted flour = 4.7 oz

1 cup granulated sugar = 8 oz = 220 g

1 cup (firmly packed) brown sugar = 6 oz = 220 g to 230 g

1 cup confectioners' sugar = 4½ oz = 115 g

1 cup honey or syrup = 12 oz

1 cup grated cheese = 4 oz

1 cup dried beans = 6 oz

1 large egg = about 2 oz or about 3 tbs

1 egg yolk = about 1 tb

1 egg white = about 2 tbs

Weight Conversions

US/UK	Metric	US/UK	Metric
½ oz	15 g	7 oz	200 g
1 oz	30 g	8 oz	250 g
1½ oz	45 g	9 oz	275 g
2 oz	60 g	10 oz	300 g
2½ oz	75 g	11 oz	325 g
3 oz	90 g	12 oz	350 g
3½ oz	100 g	13 oz	375 g
4 oz	125 g	14 oz	400 g
5 oz	150 g	15 oz	450 g
6 oz	175 g	1 lb	500 g

Liquid Conversions

US	Imperial	Metric
2 tbs	1 fl oz	30 ml
3 tbs	1¼ fl oz	45 ml
¼ cup	2 fl oz	60 ml
⅓ cup	2½ fl oz	75 ml
⅓ cup + 1 tbs	3 fl oz	90 ml
⅓ cup + 2 tbs	3½ fl oz	100 ml
½ cup	4 fl oz	125 ml
⅔ cup	5 fl oz	150 ml
¾ cup	6 fl oz	175 ml
¾ cup + 2 tbs	7 fl oz	200 ml
1 cup	8 fl oz	250 ml
1 cup + 2 tbs	9 fl oz	275 ml
1¼ cups	10 fl oz	300 ml
1⅓ cups	11 fl oz	325 ml
1½ cups	12 fl oz	350 ml
1⅔ cups	13 fl oz	375 ml
1¾ cups	14 fl oz	400 ml
1¾ cups + 2 tbs	15 fl oz	450 ml
2 cups (1 pint)	16 fl oz	500 ml
2½ cups	20 fl oz (1 pint)	600 ml
3¾ cups	1½ pints	900 ml
4 cups	1¾ pints	1 liter

Index

Note: Page references in *italics* indicate photographs.

Dipping sauces:

  garlic, 150

  ginger-sesame, 129

  honey mustard, 124

  perfectly smooth hummus, 95

  sesame-soy, 139

  spicy mayonnaise, 124

Dressings:

  Dijon vinaigrette, 99

  Thai, 104

E

Eggplant, waffled, Caprese salad with, 131–33, *133*

Eggs:

  and bacon, crispy waffled, 14–16, *15*

  bibimbaffle (waffled bibimbap), 111–13, *112*

  truffled, scrambled, and waffled, 31–33, *33*

  waffled croque madame, 49–53, *50*

  waffled Mexican migas, 118–20, *119*

  waffled tuna Niçoise salad, 66–99, *97*

F

Fawaffle (waffled falafel) and hummus, 92–95, *93*

Fish:

  waffled salmon with miso-maple glaze and asparagus, 99–101, *100*

  waffled tuna Niçoise salad, 96–99, *97*

French toast, waffled chocolate-stuffed, with whipped butter, 20–23, *21*

Fries, waffled, 151–153, *152*

Fritters, zucchini-Parmesan flattened, 145–47, *146*

Fruit. *See specific fruits*

G

Garlic dipping sauce, 150

Ginger-sesame dipping sauce, 129

Gnocchi, waffled sweet potato, 74–78, *75*

Green chile waffled quesadillas, 38–40, *39*

Greens:

  crispy sesame waffled kale, 128–30, *128*

  waffled chicken breast stuffed with spinach, pine nuts, and feta, 89–91, *91*

  waffled tuna Niçoise salad, 96–99, *97*

  WBLT (waffled bacon, lettuce, and tomato), 41–43, *42*

waffled, *87*, 89

see also specific vegetables

Vinaigrette dressing, Dijon, 99

W

Waffleburger with cheese, classic, 54–56, *55*

Waffled arancini, cheesy, 142–44, *143*

Waffled banana bread, 172–75, *173*

Waffled bibimbap (bibimbaffle), 111–13, *112*

Waffled calamari salad, 102–104, *102*

Waffled chicken breast stuffed with spinach, pine nuts, and feta, 89–91, *91*

Waffled chicken fingers, *122*, 122–24

Waffled chocolate-stuffed French toast, with whipped butter, 20–23, *21*

Waffled croque madame, 49–53, *50*

Waffled Cuban sandwich, 44–45, *45*

Waffled falafel (fawaffle) and hummus, 92–95, *93*

Waffled filet mignon, 60–62, *61*

Waffled fries, 151–53, *152*

Waffled gyro with tzatziki sauce, 46–48, *47*

Waffled ham and cheese melt with maple butter, 26–28, *27*

Waffled hash browns with rosemary, 29–31, *30*

Waffled macaroni and cheese, 67–71, *68*

Waffled meatballs, spaghetti and, 63–66, *64*

Waffled Mexican migas, 118–20, *119*

Waffled mochi with green tea ice cream, 166–69, *167*

Waffled muffins (blueberry cinnamon muffles), 23–25, *24*

Waffled oatmeal chocolate chip cookies, 163–65, *164*

Waffled onion rings, 153–55, *154*

Waffled pajeon (Korean scallion pancake), 137–39, *138*

Waffled pineapple dusted with chili powder, *160*, 160–62

Waffled portobello mushroom with Italian herbs, 57–59, *58*

Waffled recipes:
    developing your own, 191–93
    equipment for, 4–6
    naming, 192
    recipe notes, 10–11
    troubleshooting, 191–92

Waffled sage and butter sauce, 78

About the Author

Daniel Shumski is a writer and editor who has hunted ramen in Tokyo for the *Washington Post* and tracked down ice cream in Buenos Aires for the *Los Angeles Times*. Between stints at the *Chicago Sun-Times* and the *Chicago Tribune,* he worked for a Midwestern heirloom apple orchard. He lives in Montreal, where his French is a work in progress.